HOW TO WRITE ESOL MATERIALS

Kathryn Aldridge-Morris

TRAINING COURSE FOR ELT WRITERS

How To Write ESOL Materials
By Kathryn Aldridge-Morris
This edition © 2016 ELT Teacher 2 Writer
eltteacher2writer.co.uk

The author and publishers would like to thank Merton Home Tutoring Service, Patrice Palmer, Heide Wrigley and Janet Isserlis for completing questionnaires and agreeing to be interviewed for this book. We would also like to thank Patrice Palmer for giving her permission to reproduce her lesson plan on diabetes.

Contents

About The Author	5
Introduction And Aims	7
The ESOL Teaching And Learning Context	12
How Are ESOL Materials Distinct From EFL Materials? (And Why They Need To Be)	18
Writing General ESOL Materials For FE And Community Settings	21
Case Study 1: Writing A General ESOL Resource For The *ESOL Nexus* Website	28
Case Study 2: Developing An Embedded Learning Lesson Plan On Diabetes	31
Designing ESOL Resources For Museums And Art Galleries	33
Writing Materials For Voluntary One-To-One ESOL Provision	43
Adapting And Creating Materials For ESOL In Prison	51
Writing Digital Content For Low-Level ESOL Learners	58
Embedding Equality And Diversity In ESOL Materials	66
Summary Of The Writing Process	74
Commentaries On Tasks	76
References	91
Appendix 1: Introduction and Lesson Plan on Diabetes	95
Appendix 2: Questionnaires (Completed by US-based ESOL Materials Developers)	108

About The Author

I'm a freelance teacher trainer, writer and editor, and have worked in the field of English Language Teaching (ELT) for 18 years.

I started out in publishing in 2002 by writing A level Spanish textbooks and teacher books, and began writing for ELT when I was an ESOL tutor for Bristol Community Education Service. I was commissioned by Bristol City Museum and Art Gallery to produce materials for 'The Stuff of Life': a National Gallery touring exhibition. The Museum wanted to have a more inclusive reach and won Heritage Lottery funding to create resources that could be used to draw ESOL classes out of the classroom and into the museum.

After going freelance full-time, I worked as a consultant for the British Council, first as a Resource Specialist, then taking on the role of a Project Coordinator, commissioning and editing resources for the British Council's ESOL

Nexus website. The resources span a range of projects including low level and beginner's ESOL, and materials to support ESOL teachers in prisons. The role involved writing, commissioning and editing lesson plans, interactive CPD modules, teacher's packs, online self-access resources using authoring tools, and writing scripts for the original videos embedded in these. I worked for eight months on the ESOL Offender Learning project, which involved visiting prisons and running workshops for ESOL practitioners in custodial settings.

I've also been working as a digital and print author for several publishers, including Oxford University Press. I've authored materials for the Oxford Online Skills Program, shortlisted for the 2014 English-Speaking Union's President's Award, online practice materials and test banks for the digital components of several OUP courses, such as *Solutions*, *Directions* and *Insight*, and have written and contributed to student workbooks.

If you would like to get in touch, please email k.aldridgemorris@live.co.uk

Introduction And Aims

WHAT IS ESOL?

ESOL is distinct from other strands of English Language Teaching (ELT) and it also differs around the world. In the UK, ESOL means *English for Speakers of Other Languages*. ESOL learners are migrants settling and working in the UK, and comprise new arrivals as well as long-term residents.

English language education for adult migrants in other English-language speaking countries such as the US, Canada and Australia is often described as ESL (*English as a Second Language*). Definitions are further muddied because this term also often encompasses what would be considered *EFL* provision in the UK; that is *English as a Foreign Language* for students on short-term study visas. The US website *eslfocus.com* describes the distinction as being:

ESL – English as a second language – English language programs in English-speaking countries.
EFL – English as a foreign language – English language programs in non-English-speaking countries.

ESOL is different to other types of ELT provision in the extent to which it is determined by the socio- and geo-political context in which it is delivered. And this, of course, varies around the world too. The local ESOL classroom is impacted by global migration patterns and trends. For example, in the UK there has been an increase in the number of ESOL learners from EU accession countries (e.g. Poland and Hungary) in the past decade. The top two countries of origin and asylum in Australia in 2013 were Afghanistan and Syria (Refugee Council of Australia) and in the US the largest proportion of immigrants are from Mexico (Migration Policy Institute). And one current trend in Canada is that the government is actively recruiting healthcare professionals from India to meet a skills shortage in the healthcare system. So we see a varied ESOL landscape, with all sorts of factors in play.

Therefore, while much of the focus of this book is on ESOL in the UK, the approach (which takes the context-specific needs of learners as the starting point) will be relevant to educationalists working in migration contexts in other English-speaking countries. I suggest that ESOL materials are most effective when they are designed to meet local needs, based upon a solid understanding of local teaching and learning contexts. By definition then, they won't always have the global reach of for example, EFL materials that have been written for foreign students working towards internationally recognised qualifications. That said, migrants wanting to acquire English language skills, as part of the process of settling in their host country, will need to engage in the same types of language and literacy practices, and similarly need to learn how to deal with new systems, bureaucracies and institutions. You'll be able therefore to take the underlying principles and apply them to migrant teaching and learning contexts outside the UK.

ESOL MATERIALS

ESOL materials come in a range of formats. They can be printed resources or online resources, lesson plans written for teachers to use in class, or to support informal learning outside the classroom, materials for one-to-one tuition, course books, CPD, self-study packs, online self-access learning objects[1], or apps[2]. This book will explore some of the main issues related to writing for ESOL, by looking at the process of materials design for particular ESOL contexts.

It's an integrated skills approach and so the book is not organised around the development of discrete skills. I discuss how materials work well when developed in response to the needs of learners in specific ESOL settings. There are suggestions for tasks and activities which facilitate the kinds of interactions that allow for real language learning to happen.

First and foremost, I want this book to offer an overview of ESOL and practical ideas on how to write ESOL materials. For anyone wanting to delve deeper into the theories of second language acquisition or materials development, these will be signposted as we go along and there is a full reference list on page 91. There will also be some overlap with the content in other books in this series, and I will refer you to these too. This book will not explain how to write specific activity types, rather how to use your understanding of the different ESOL teaching and learning contexts to write materials that meet learner needs and to design online content that is accessible.

---

[1] **learning object** An online activity. In online learning design you divide all the resources you are creating into learning objects.

[2] **app** Short for 'application', which is a synonym for computer program. The word 'app' refers to applications that run on mobile devices. Not to be confused with a prison application form, which is also referred to in abbreviated form.

The main aims of this book are

- to consider the specific characteristics of a range of ESOL learning and teaching settings, and to explore the implications of these for the development of learner-centred resources.
- to consider some overarching principles for the design of ESOL materials in the context of specific case studies.
- to explore how ESOL differs from mainstream ELT and think about how these differences can inform our approach to writing.
- to help you consider ways of evaluating the materials that already exist and using this as a starting point for your own materials development.
- to discuss the issues around creating online self-access resources for learners who have low levels of English and emerging ICT skills.
- to consider what it means for a resource to support 'inclusive' teaching practice and how we can write materials that are informed by the UK Equality Act 2010.

Who is this book for?

- Newly qualified ESOL tutors who would like a deeper understanding of the process of materials development.
- Experienced ESOL tutors who need to develop their own materials because their existing resources do not meet their learners' needs (such as ESOL teachers in prisons, or volunteer ESOL tutors working one-to-one) or who want to diversify into writing for publication.
- Teachers who've identified a gap in provision and want to disseminate their resources in order to build capacity

in their area of ESOL, and contribute to raising standards in teaching and learning.
- Authors of mainstream ELT materials who want to write for the ESOL market.
- Writers and teachers wanting to create digital ESOL content.

NOTE

This book focuses on materials development for adult learners.

All the opinions expressed in this book are my own. My words do not represent the views of my current or former employers.

Proceeds from the royalties made from this book will be donated to the charity the Refugee Council, supporting and empowering refugees.

The ESOL Teaching And Learning Context

Before an author starts writing, there will have been a great deal of research undertaken into target learner characteristics and the teaching and learning context. If you have been commissioned to write, the editor will give you a clear brief. If you are designing the materials yourself, this book will serve as a useful starting point for this research and suggest a framework for using your research to create learner-centred resources.

Task 1

1 Take a few minutes to make a list of the different contexts where ESOL learning and teaching takes place in the UK or other English-speaking countries.

2 Who are ESOL learners?

Compare your answers with the commentary on page 76.

It is important that you are clear about who you are writing for at the outset. This will have implications for the materials you develop; first in terms of content and second in terms of design. As we have seen, ESOL takes place in a huge range of settings, and some of them are not designed foremost for adult learning. You'll need to consider the constraints of the learning environment. But also don't forget to consider the resources that can be exploited in the surroundings. We'll think about this as we consider the settings in more detail. The more you take into account the learners and teachers and the way they work, the better your materials will meet their needs and expectations.

You may have identified a specialist area of ESOL that you want to write for, and a few of these are discussed in the other sections. Let's think for the moment about some generic characteristics of ESOL before considering how to write general ESOL materials to support teaching in mainstream adult and community settings and FE.

MOTIVES FOR LEARNING ENGLISH

First let's consider the range of motivations of ESOL learners in the UK.

'ESOL learners do not usually come to the UK primarily in order to improve their English, but for a range of other reasons – political, economic or personal. They may be refugees or economic migrants; they may have arrived recently, or have been living in the UK for a long period; they may have a high level of previous education, or have never been to school.

Most ESOL learners are not learning English as an end in itself, but because they want to do other things which require an improved knowledge of English; such as work, study, participate more fully in UK life and support their children's learning.'

ESOL is therefore 'more than a language' (NIACE[3], 2006). You'll need to consider the *content* of the material as much as you will the target language forms. This content should enable you to embed i) broader learning aims that address the range of social and personal issues learners bring to the

---

[3] **NIACE** (National Institute of Adult Continuing Education) was an educational charity in England and Wales dedicated to promoting adult learning. In 2016 it merged with the Centre for Economic and Social Inclusion to form the Learning and Work Institute.

classroom and ii) the achievement of 'soft outcomes'. 'Soft' outcomes differ from 'hard' outcomes, such as gaining a qualification or getting a job, and are less easily measurable. Yet, they are an integral part of ESOL provision, which often positions itself as a social enterprise or a site for social change and political activism.

'For many, confidence in English language opens doors and helps people engage in and contribute to civil society. Lack of fluency in the language condemns many people to poverty. ESOL is both a subject in its own right and a means to an end for individuals. … the opportunity to improve English language should be a right; a chance to contribute to and at the same time shape the communities in which we live and work.' (NIACE, 2006)

Task 2

What are some 'soft outcomes' for ESOL learners?

Compare your answers with the commentary on page 76.

Your materials will be more robust if they can incorporate learning outcomes that address these wider personal and social needs, and not simply centre on language acquisition. In specialised fields of ESOL you should also search for context-specific outcomes.

One way into this is to consider all of the 'stakeholders' involved in the context you are writing for. For example, let's consider ESOL in prison. Here there are not only the prisoners and teachers to consider but also prison officers, civilian staff, the families of prisoners, as well as society as a whole who stand to benefit from prisoners speaking better English. How can your resources address the needs of these other stakeholders? And the more stakeholders that stand to benefit from your materials, the more impact they will have and the more funding you can draw down for them.

CHARACTERISTICS OF THE ESOL CLASSROOM

As touched on earlier, in many respects the ESOL classroom can be seen as a microcosm of wider global events. Eleven years ago I had one class that comprised largely Pakistani and Sudanese women, a Colombian political refugee and an Iraqi general. Another class was predominantly made up of Somali and Congolese learners. Not all were refugees and asylum seekers; some had come to join their spouses and been in the country for many years. However, they'd lived in closed communities and had low levels of English. Several years later, there were more Spanish, Lithuanian and Polish learners in classes. The picture also varies across the UK and constantly changes in response to shifts in migration patterns and domestic policies such as dispersal[4].

The term *superdiversity* first coined by Vertovec (2006) and subsequently employed by others, for example (Baynham et al., 2007) and (Hann et al, 2010), describes the heterogeneous make-up of the ESOL classroom. ESOL classes are strikingly diverse in terms of motivation for learning English, nationality, educational and cultural backgrounds, spiky profiles[5], learner expectations, life experience and length of stay in the UK, amongst other things. This *superdiversity* translates into an extremely

---

[4] **dispersal** UK government scheme to move asylum seekers outside London and the south east of England. Policies such as these have come in for criticism as they can lead to isolation and discrimination.

[5] **spiky profile** When a student has different levels in reading, writing, speaking and listening. For example, they might be at Entry 3 for speaking but have Entry 1 writing skills.

challenging teaching and learning context. This is compounded by the complex problems learners bring to the classroom; many may be living with stress and trauma, be waiting for immigration decisions and come from communities that are likely to be in poverty.

Classes are also more likely to be mixed level, with pre-entry[6] learners working alongside Entry 3[7] learners, or learners with no or low literacy levels studying with confident learners who have been through formal schooling and achieved exams in their own country.

All in all, it is a less than ideal teaching and learning set-up, and no amount of outstanding teaching or innovative resourcing can always cater for this. However, good materials will display an awareness of the constraints, and indeed opportunities, that this superdiversity brings.

Task 3
What implications do these features of a 'typical' general ESOL class have for materials design?
- superdiversity   - mixed-level classes
- length of stay in the UK
- the complex social and personal problems and issues that learners are dealing with

Compare your answers with the commentary on page 77.

---

[6] **pre-entry** The level before Entry 1. There is some controversy surrounding the use of this term as it is used by literacy teachers to describe learners with learning difficulties.

[7] **Entry 3** One of the national standards of English language proficiency as defined by the Adult ESOL Core Curriculum. It is roughly aligned with the CEFR level B1. At this level, ESOL learners' spoken competence is often much better than their literacy skills.

It's important to write your resource for a particular level as defined in the Adult ESOL Core Curriculum[8], with teacher's notes to support differentiation for other levels in the class. Clearly label the resource so that teachers can find it easily or search for it quickly online. You should also map resources to the Scottish Credit and Qualifications Framework (SCQF) as well as to the Qualifications Credit Framework (QCF) for England, Wales and Northern Ireland. See *accreditedqualifications.org.uk/qualifications-and-credit-framework-qcf.html* to see how they equate.

For writers developing materials for outside the UK, you'll need to first find out whether the ESOL provision is accredited. Then you'll need to research the nationally recognised framework that the qualifications are mapped to and reference these in your resources.

Further reading
Aldridge-Morris, K. (2016) The learners that publishers forgot. *MaWSIG Blog*, IATEFL
mawsig.iatefl.org/the-learners-that-publishers-forgot

---

[8] **Adult ESOL Core Curriculum** This is the national curriculum for Adult ESOL in England, Wales and Northern Ireland, devised in 2001 as part of the *Skills for Life* policy (a national strategy for improving adult literacy, numeracy and ESOL). It is based upon the National Standards for Adult Literacy. It defines proficiency in English based on the component skills needed for reading, writing, speaking and listening at five levels: Entry 1, Entry 2, Entry 3, Level 1 and Level 2. There are key grammatical structures at each level of the core curriculum. More information about how ESOL qualifications are aligned with the international Common European Framework (CEF) levels can be found on the Accredited Qualifications website, *accreditedqualifications.org.uk*.

How Are ESOL Materials Distinct From EFL Materials?
(And Why They Need To Be)

An important first step when you are writing is to conduct an audit of the resources that are currently out there, evaluate them and then work out gaps in the provision. For all kinds of reasons, EFL materials are often used in ESOL contexts. This can lead to a disconnect between the English-speaking world presented on the pages (or on-screen) and the lives of the learners. This can be disengaging, demotivating and limit opportunities for meaningful personalisation activities. 'The most important thing the learning materials have to do is to help the learner to connect the learning experience in the classroom to their own life outside the course.' (Tomlinson, 2013:25)

One of the reasons that EFL materials are inappropriate is that they do not transmit a world view that is pertinent to the vast majority of refugees or asylum seekers who have come to settle in the UK. Nor do they address the wider needs of migrant groups looking to settle and work in the UK, reflect their reality or aspirations.

'…they do not speak directly to their interests or concerns and often serve merely as the vehicle to practise "target language"…' (Bryers et al., 2014:38)

Consider one prison teacher I met at a workshop I delivered on materials development last year. She told me that she'd got *Cutting Edge* to use in class and had been stumped when it came to the question, practising the second conditional – 'If you won the lottery, where would you go on holiday?' It was a Category B prison and most of the learners in her class were in for a minimum of ten years.

Task 4

1 What resources do you currently use? Were they written for the EFL or ESOL market?

2 In which ways do you think EFL and ESOL materials differ from each other?

Compare your answers with the commentary on page 78.

EFL and ESOL materials are different because they are written for different types of students or learners, studying in different settings with different motivations for learning English. When I've had a brief to write EFL materials, it's generally based upon a controlled grammar and skills syllabus. I'm given a document with the scope of the grammar and lexis and told to write texts that contextualise these items in an engaging way that will appeal to a certain age of student, studying in a certain country.

Several EFL publishers use wordlists and vocabulary databases, such as the English Vocabulary Profile (EVP) (Cambridge English) and the Oxford 3000™ (Oxford University Press). These are based on research into the frequency of vocabulary as it's actually used by students in exam papers, for example, and native speakers. The EVP then ranks the words according to CEFR levels.

The EVP lists what learners are already supposed to know at a certain level. Lists such as these are used as a reference source in EFL, in order to select target lexis for materials and syllabus design and for authors to use as a benchmark for their writing. This approach is somewhat inadequate for ESOL materials development however. First, it's based largely on written language. Second, it's very prescriptive in terms of the vocabulary editors will allow you to use in your input texts, and you can find words that are deemed to be at too high a level being edited out. Migrants settling in the UK need the language immediately, in order to make sense of and get on with their new lives. As one colleague said to me, 'My learners don't have the luxury of living in a world surrounded only by Entry 1 level vocabulary'. I'll suggest below how it's more appropriate to extrapolate lexical items from the authentic texts that learners need to engage with every day, with a view to grading the tasks, not the key language. Where you *will* be able to make use of wordlists that rank words according to CEFR levels, is in the writing of rubrics. (See *Writing digital content for low-level learners*, page 58.)

What effective EFL and ESOL materials do have in common is that they will be informed chiefly by the writer's classroom experience of what works and doesn't work for different learners in specific contexts. They will also be underpinned by theories of second language acquisition, materials development and pedagogy. Please see the References section for further reading. See the other titles in the *ELT Teacher 2 Writer* series for an in-depth look at specific aspects of ELT materials writing.

My own approach has derived as much from my teaching experience and from feedback from editors and piloters, as it has from academic reading. And it's an approach that continues to evolve and that I continue to fine-tune as I learn more from new editors and hear back from different students. In places I refer to some theories of second language acquisition, to show my rationale for the design of specific tasks, in the different sections below. I'll also talk about how some successful resources are often based largely on the intuition of the experienced teacher.

Writing General ESOL Materials For FE And Community Settings

There is an increasing trend towards learner-centredness in ESOL teaching practice and this has led to participatory approaches such as *Reflect,* in which materials and class themes are generated by the learners in situ. To explore this approach further and consider participatory tools as inspiration for some of your own materials development, visit the *Reflect* website (*www.reflect-action.org/resources*).

Although learner-*generated* resources and content are arguably the ideal springboard for a learner-centred experience, there will always be the demand for ESOL resources from busy, new or less confident teachers. This section looks at meeting the demand for ESOL materials from FE or community providers.

Addressing everyday needs that arise from low levels of English

Simpson and Cooke (2015) describe publicly-funded ESOL provision as typically comprising 'survival ESOL', 'ESOL for work' and 'ESOL for citizenship'. In some respects, this book focuses largely on 'survival' ESOL, because it looks at creating resources that meet the needs of learners who are settling in the UK and other English-speaking countries, (or settled but with low levels of English), and who need to understand 'the system' in order to get by. This book hopes to foster a 'critical' approach to needs analysis, i.e. generating content in response to what *teachers* and *learners* say they need.

In the same chapter, Simpson and Cooke discuss post-war ESOL classes:

'ESL materials were home-produced at first and heavily functional, dealing with basic survival and adjustment to life in the new country ...'

They discuss how this approach came in for criticism for presenting 'unreal' situations and more recently the 'problem-free representations of everyday experiences' (ibid) that appear in the ESOL Skills for Life materials. I would add that it's not simply that the situations are 'problem-free' but that they are fairly *safe* or *superficial*. By this I mean that they don't reflect the full picture of life for many learners. ESOL materials are full of visits to the doctor, but how often do we see health issues that go beyond common ailments? Where are the materials to help learners acquire the language to understand and describe mental health issues or FGM[9] or childhood disabilities?

The number of new arrivals to the UK continues to grow and the need to 'survive' still exists. It's an approach that's still valid therefore, but for it to be effective and empowering, the language and texts need to be realistic. Language should be 'authentic in the sense that it represents how the language is typically used. If the language is inauthentic because it has been written or reduced to exemplify a particular language feature, then the learners will not acquire the ability to use the language typically or effectively.' (Tomlinson, 2010) This is especially important for ESOL learners who are typically in a disadvantaged social position and who routinely need to negotiate bureaucratic institutions. Yet, '... corpus based

---

[9] **FGM** Female genital mutilation. Over 66,000 women and girls living in Britain have experienced FGM. (NHS, 2015)

studies have identified a linguistic gap between commercial materials and the actual language use.' (Harwood, 2010:9) It's important to thoroughly research the area that you are designing tasks about, in order to mine it for authentic language use. Roberts and Cooke (2009) state that 'materials should ... exemplify the social relations and discourse routines of everyday and institutional interactions.' Where possible try to record and transcribe genuine spoken English and interactions, and base listening texts that you write on these.

Where to start?

The first step is to use your intuition and experience as a classroom teacher, and your knowledge of the sector and *specific* teaching context, to choose an overarching theme or topic. This will contextualise the language learning in a way that is meaningful to your learners, and will lead to wider learning outcomes, through learners engaging with content that is intrinsically interesting and motivating.

Next research relevant, authentic, spoken and written texts. *From these texts*, extrapolate key vocabulary, grammar structures, functions and skills that you want to work with. It's important that you don't overwhelm beginner learners with difficult authentic texts that won't have graded language. Either adapt the text, without detracting from the authenticity (this is where your skill as a writer comes in), or carefully grade the task, perhaps focussing on features of the text such as layout, or headings.

Alternatively, if you choose to take a lexical set as your starting point, say 'colours' for an entry level class, find a text that contextualises different colours. Try to ensure this is innovative and will lead to wider learner outcomes. For example, the spoken text could be a supermarket worker describing a lost child over a tannoy and this contextualises the different colours in clothing and physical description, but also embeds listening skills and introduces learners to a specific social practice that exists in the community.

We used this approach for a similar concept for one of the *ESOL Nexus* Beginner's modules that I coordinated. *Lost child*, written by Catrin Ashton, is a self-study module (with accompanying lesson plan for use in class – see *https://goo.gl/GJF7lS*) with an embedded video, based on a woman called Faduma whose son goes missing in a supermarket. Listening skills, language work (spelling rules for adding -*ing*) and vocabulary for describing people (colour, clothing, hair) is practised in this context. Learners are also exposed to question forms in context. Comprehension questions are also included that develop visual literacy, as well as listening skills – an important advantage of using video in class.

Maybe you want to take language functions as your starting point. You could take the list of functions of a particular level and think of a situation and related texts to contextualise it. These will generate your learner-centred tasks and activities. For example, here is a list of the communicative functions at Entry 1 (DfES, 2001):

> give personal information; ask for personal information; introduce family and close friends; tell the time/day, etc.; ask the time/day; express ability; enquire about ability; say when you do not understand; ask for clarification; check back; correct; spell words aloud; describe places and things; give information as part of a simple explanation; give single-step directions and instructions; make requests – ask for directions; enquire about prices and quantities; make requests – ask for something; make requests – ask someone to do

something; respond to a request; express likes and dislikes; express feelings; express wishes; express views; agree and disagree; apologise; express a preference; express thanks; greet; respond to greetings; describe health and symptoms; invite and offer; accept; decline; take leave

Can you find a new angle or an innovative way to contextualise one of these functions, in an everyday scenario or typical encounter that your learners will relate to?

Task 5 has a series of questions that can be used as a framework to help you i) evaluate existing materials, and ii) reflect on how you might adapt them or create your own in response to gaps in the content. There's no commentary as it's designed to get you to reflect on the process.

Task 5

There are many resources based on the topic of schools and education in ESOL materials. Find two or three.

1 What are the strengths and weaknesses of the resources? Are the materials engaging?

2 Are there any gaps in the content?

3 Can you think of a more innovative or more 'authentic' way to present the language?

4 Could you think of a way to adapt the materials for other levels or for a different mode of delivery (i.e. online, as an app, in print)?

Task 6 provides you with the opportunity to get your creative juices flowing and to start to think about the development of a specific resource.

Task 6

Take the topic of food as your starting point. Think of one authentic written text that you could use to create a resource for an ESOL class for parents in a Sure Start children's centre[10].

Compare your answers with the commentary on page 81.

For detailed advice on designing speaking, listening, reading and writing activities, please see the other titles in the *ELT Teacher 2 Writer* series.

Make sure that you pilot your resources and amend according to any insightful feedback. This critical stage will not only improve the quality of your resource but will help you to reflect and develop as a writer.

A final note. You should bear in mind that 'To sustain long-term motivation, materials need to go beyond survival needs and … offer opportunities for personal and professional growth …' (Hann et al., 2010). And Tomlinson (2013) states that: 'The most important result that learning materials can achieve is to engage the emotions of the learners.' Therefore, consider creating

---

[10] **Sure Start children's centres** Children's centres that were set up (as part of the Labour Party's Sure Start initiative in 1998) in order to improve outcomes for young children and their families, especially those from deprived backgrounds and disadvantaged areas, and with the goal of reducing child poverty. They have been compared to the Head Start programme in the US and Australia. Austerity cuts in the UK have led to a significant number of closures of Sure Start centres in the past few years.

content that is also affectively engaging[11], as well as using subject matter that is intrinsically motivating through meeting learners' real-life needs.

For inspiration see the freely downloadable Easier English Wiki 'ready lessons' published by the New Internationalist (*eewiki.newint.org/index.php/Ready_Lessons*).

---

[11] **affective engagement** This is when the language learning process involves the feelings and emotions of learners to promote deeper learning. Learner affect relates to engagement, motivation and confidence. Activities that encourage personal responses are affectively engaging.

Case Study 1: Writing A General ESOL Resource For The *ESOL Nexus* Website

CHOOSING THE TOPIC

As part of the application to become a Resource Specialist for the British Council, I was invited to create a downloadable ESOL worksheet for the *ESOL Nexus* project. I wasn't creating it for a specific class, it was to be published on the website and therefore I needed to take into consideration the wider ESOL landscape.

I decided to create a worksheet based on the topic of school for Entry 1 learners. There were several reasons for this choice. The first stemmed from my teaching experience. Most of my learners were from the Somali community in Bristol and classes were predominantly women, and these women were overwhelmingly mothers with pre-school and school age children. This reflected the wider picture in England. In 2010 there were 187,000 adult ESOL learners recorded and of these 66% were women and 25% of those had children under the age of seven. (Action for ESOL, 2011)

I've always been interested in the school playground as one of the primary sites of social integration. This is clearly an area in which poor language skills lead to social exclusion; the inability of parents to fully participate in their child's school life has a detrimental effect on the child's education, as well as the parent's increased feelings of alienation and loneliness.

I also drew on my own observations as a parent. I observed that on a 'dress-down day' or a 'welly day', children whose parents did not speak English were coming to school dressed in uniform or school shoes. The effect on a child missing out, being 'different' because they're wearing something different, is huge and adds to a sense of otherness and exclusion. Not to mention the poor parent whose child's shoes are ruined because they needed wellies that day.

DESIGNING THE WORKSHEET

I chose the most common school items as the vocabulary set for the lesson plan and included dialectical forms such as *daps* with footnotes to standard English. (Of course, if you were writing for EFL materials for international students abroad, you'd never have regional variations as your target lexis, only standard forms.)

The meaning of key words was elicited with the use of photos, and these were photos I'd taken myself. (Be careful if taking your own photos of schools/pupils, etc. and do seek permission from both the school and pupils first.) In this instance, professional photo libraries were useless in terms of finding 'book bags' that are used in the real world – all I could find online were backpacks and 'old-school' satchels. It was equally difficult finding lunchboxes with food that didn't look like it had just been prepared by middle-class British parents for a baking competition.

USING AN AUTHENTIC TEXT-BASED APPROACH

The worksheet was accepted and adapted into a online self-study resource for learners. (This was followed up by a lesson plan that was designed to enable teachers to work through the online module with the whole group in class. See *esol.britishcouncil.org/content/teachers/lessons-and-activities/teaching-beginners/reading-texts-school.*) For the online module, I decided to contextualise the language items in the format of text messages. I observed that phone texts from school were the most typical way that the school communicated with parents. I wanted the mode of language use to be authentic as well as the target language.

I downloaded all of the texts that I had received in the last year from school and from these I identified recurring themes; namely notifications of dress-down days, whole school walks with wellies, nits in the class and invitations to assemblies or class events. I compared with parents at other schools across the country; they were all fairly formulaic. I then extrapolated key vocabulary from the texts and recurring grammar structures, such as use of the imperative. Finally, I wrote three texts based upon those I'd downloaded. In order to keep them authentic I kept non-standard vocabulary items (such as *wellies*) and informal features of texting language, such as ellipsis[12].

The learning aims were framed by the learning of these key words, reading and understanding the gist of school texts, selecting detail from texts (for example, finding assembly times; finding out whether it was addressed to a particular year group) and using strategies to guess the meaning of unknown words in texts. I wanted learners to be able to transfer this strategy to their everyday reading of genuine text messages.

The Year 2 ESOL Nexus Monitoring and Evaluation report stated that this resource was the sixth most popular on the website, which hosts over 1,000 resources for teachers and learners. I guess the lesson here is that it's our intuition as experienced ESOL teachers and in-depth knowledge of our learners that best informs the kind of materials that learners will engage with.

---

[12] **ellipsis** The omission of words

Case Study 2: Developing An Embedded Learning Lesson Plan On Diabetes

India and China are currently regarded as being 'the diabetes capitals of the world'. The *diabetes.co.uk* website goes on to explain that type 2 diabetes is up to six times more likely in people of South Asian descent and three times more likely in African and Africa-Caribbean people.

Patrice Palmer is a Canadian ESL teacher based in Hamilton. One of the resources that she has developed is a lesson plan on diabetes. While she was researching the disease following her son's diagnosis, Palmer realised that her learners were a high-risk group. She explained to me that 'ESL colleagues downtown felt it was like an epidemic'. Moreover, not everyone had a family doctor willing, or able, to explain the complexities of the disease to non-native speakers.

'Research suggests that immigrants arrive in Canada healthier than the average Canadian, (known as 'the healthy immigrant effect'), however, within a short period of time (five to seven years) their health declines.' (De Maio and Kemp, 2010; cited in Palmer, 2015: see Appendix 1, page 95)

She undertook some research and found that there wasn't anything on diabetes in ESL teaching materials and so identified the need for a resource. She researched core information and adapted the language to make it accessible to ESL learners.

LINC (Language Instruction for Newcomers to Canada) provides free government-funded language classes to refugees and asylum seekers. One of the themes of the LINC programme is health and Palmer linked her lesson plan to this in the curriculum. It was pitched at Level 4 of the Canadian Language Benchmarks (CLB. See *language.ca*), the equivalent to the ESOL Core Curriculum in the UK.

It's an embedded learning approach which combines the acquisition of language skills with the learning about health. Palmer views the ESL classroom as 'a site for health literacy and language learning'. The learning objectives of the lesson plan reference CLB language learning objectives, as well as the wider learning aims of raising awareness of the symptoms of diabetes and promoting discussion on healthy living, with the aim of reducing the risks of developing type 2 diabetes in high-risk ethnic populations. The lesson plan was piloted with colleagues and more than 300 adult learners, and has received positive feedback – Palmer hopes to extend it into a course in the future.

See Appendix 1 (page 95) for Palmer's Introduction and photocopiable lesson plan on diabetes.

Designing ESOL Resources For Museums And Art Galleries

There are so many possibilities for all kinds of ESOL resources for museums and art galleries. The aim of this section is to get you considering these possibilities and to suggest how to turn creative teaching and learning ideas into resources that can be adapted for local museums.

You might want to write resources to facilitate a visit to your local museum and these could be for a temporary or permanent exhibition, paper-based or online (if you want to reach a wider audience). Your resources will almost be like a template with ideas for activities and an overarching framework. These ought to include the worksheets that the learners will be working with during the visit and accompanying teacher's notes that could be in the form of lesson plans and additional resources such as flashcards or questionnaire templates for pre- and post-visit sessions. The materials could be based on a specific theme or you could provide a framework for teachers to work with the themes that arise from the learners themselves.

On the other hand, you may have been commissioned to write, in which case you'll negotiate content and format to produce bespoke materials for your museum.

Supporting informal learning opportunities outside the classroom

Just as ESOL resources designed for specific educational settings are much more than simply tools for language acquisition, the same applies to materials we write to support educational visits to museums and art galleries.

ESOL resources are never an end in themselves; here they are a starting point for, amongst other things:

- moving the learning outside of the classroom,
- encouraging learners to tell their stories,
- helping learners better understand their place in the world.

'Some literacy, numeracy and ESOL learners have little or no first-hand experience of life outside their immediate neighbourhood. Others have a poor understanding of where they are in the UK ...The best solution is to reinforce existing knowledge using trips out and other exploratory activities ... provide information on the additional resources and facilities available in the community so that learners can extend their neighbourhood and geographic knowledge beyond the learning environment ... providing good opportunities for intensive learning and developing social skills, as well as widening learners' horizons in many other ways.'(DfES, 2002)

In this section I want to suggest ideas for creating resources that are based on objects and images housed in museums and art galleries. I'll also think about how the materials lead to wider learning and social outcomes.

MUSEUM OBJECTS

Museums are full of other people's stories that lie behind the objects on exhibit. Objects hold meanings and are not just decoration; these possessions reveal the character of those who own or owned them. ESOL resources can be designed to get learners thinking about the characters behind objects, finding objects that speak to them and that perhaps represent something about themselves. It's an opportunity for learners to make cross-cultural connections between objects, and between *themselves* and the stories behind the objects. In this way we can draw on learners' own experiences and truly personalise the learning experience. It's also a means of promoting cross-cultural understanding and in the longer term contributing to social cohesion in the community.

I will look at a few different ways that museum objects can be used to stimulate discussion, learning and the development of 'soft' outcomes.

SCOPING YOUR MUSEUM RESOURCES

Task 7

Think of the *type* of activities that you could include in resources for:

1 pre-visit
2 the visit
3 post-visit

to your local museum.

Compare your answers with the commentary on page 81.

MAKING CROSS-CULTURAL CONNECTIONS

My thanks to the Iroko Theatre Company whose inspiring workshop at the British Museum informed my first activity here.

One idea would be to produce a worksheet that could be laminated and cut up and used as flashcards. You'd write instructions in the teacher's notes or an accompanying lesson plan. The procedure would involve distributing the cards to small groups of three or four learners who then look around the gallery for an object or image that they associate with the word on that card. They regroup and on another worksheet provided in the pack collate their ideas. In order for the learners to make cross-cultural connections, this task could be carried out across different galleries exhibiting objects from different regions.

Task 8

Think of six words or concepts that could be used in the activity described above and hence as a springboard for cross-cultural discussion.

Compare your answers with the commentary on page 82.

FINDING PERSONAL MEANINGS IN OBJECTS

An alternative could be to take a specific *object*, as opposed to concept, as the starting point of a language task. I'll discuss one example below to show how we can use objects to facilitate extremely powerful and transformative learning experiences.

Thrones, chairs and stools are recurring objects in art and the everyday. They can connote status as well as holding very personal meaning. Here are some examples. The British Museum has a collection of elaborate 19th century stools from Nigeria carved with various motifs of wealth and power, such as weapons and animal horns. I was also drawn to the *ancestral* stools on display. Here is the blurb from one exhibit in the British Museum's Wellcome Gallery:

'In Akan societies stools have an important role as both regalia and symbols of power. A royal or title-holder's office is represented by a wooden stool carved in their honour and used at ceremonies. Each stool is closely related to its owner's personality and soul (kra). A stool owner who has had a worthy life and who died in office will have his or her stool 'blackened' in a special ceremony some time after the funeral. The corpse is usually placed on the stool to be washed before it is dressed and adorned. After the funeral, the deceased's hair and nail clippings are placed in the hole that runs vertically through the central column of the stool.'

Chairs and stools are not just significant in other cultures and at other times. I was recently staying at a hotel in Brighton that had acquired Winston Churchill's favourite chair. Every adult that saw it, and then saw who it had belonged to, felt compelled to have a go at sitting on it!

I was commissioned by Bristol Museum and Art Gallery to write a set of resources for Entry 3 learners, visiting *The Stuff of Life* National Gallery touring exhibition. I was drawn to two distinct and powerful representations of chairs and thrones that I selected as the focus of part of the course pack. The first was a painting: Van Gogh's Chair, 1888 by Vincent van Gogh. The second was a sculpture: The Throne of Weapons, 2001 by Kestor. This was a throne created with the guns that had been exchanged for tools, when the civil war in Mozambique ended in 1992.

Experienced ESOL practitioners understand that 'talk is work' (Baynham et al., 2007:8) and these objects were the springboard for much discussion; political and personal. I designed resources that facilitated discussion before, during and after the visit, encouraging the learners to think about different art forms, the meaning behind these objects, and their personal responses to them. None of the tasks were designed to get the learners using the museum to find information, rather to use language to express opinions and feelings.

I piloted the materials in two of my own classes. The learners discussed the significance of choosing to turn the decommissioned weapons into a throne. The sculpture itself evoked powerful associations for many learners. There were some follow-up discussions, one based on the fact that none of the weapons used during the civil war had been made in Africa. This was information they'd elicited from the exhibition themselves and the theme had emerged from the visit.

As a follow-up activity, I created a worksheet with the aim of encouraging learners to make personal associations with the objects. There were images of many different chairs and learners were asked to say which chair they would be and why:

'I am an easy chair. A rocking chair. Going backwards and forwards, backwards and forwards.'
Faduma, Entry 3 class, Bristol Community Education

'The folding chair represents my life. Ready to go. I don't know where I'm going to be at any time. Will I go back to Africa or stay in England? I just always have to be ready to pack up and go. I'm folded up, ready to go.'
Raqiya, Entry 3 class, Bristol Community Education

These were tasks that successfully encouraged talk at the level of discourse and developed speaking skills. '…where learners were 'speaking from within' they produced longer, more complex stretches of talk, which we know to be essential for language learning and acquisition to take place.' (Cooke and Roberts, 2007:2)

Task 9
Think of other everyday objects that could be the theme of an ESOL museum resource.

Compare your answers with the commentary on page 83.

A third focus for the learning and teaching activities in your resources could be the symbols and motifs found on objects and in paintings. This is a wonderful way to generate cross-cultural discussion and elicit responses and opinions. The learning themes and the creative possibilities are endless. I'd recommend producing pre-visit resources that support the teacher with pre-teaching the concept of *symbol* and representation.

Here are some ideas:

Colour and the meaning that different cultures attach to colours
I wrote a reading text on this theme for Oxford University Press's *Online Skills Program* and considered the use of colour in idioms around the world to express emotions such as fear or anger. It was fascinating to see how this differed. (I would have guessed that the Brazilian 'yellow smile' was one masking fear, but I'd have been wrong. If someone gives you a yellow smile in Brazil, it's a false smile.)

You could think about the colour of clothes at different life events and create tasks based upon this, as part of a pre-visit resource pack.

Materials that objects are made from
Here is another blurb from the British Museum's Wellcome Gallery (these blurbs are excellent springboards for creativity): 'In traditional Palestinian culture certain natural materials and specific colours had medicinal or protective

qualities. The charms, necklaces and amulets worn by the Palestinian village women and the nomadic Bedouin of the desert usually incorporated one or more of these elements. These natural materials included tortoise shells to ensure longevity or white stone beads for new mothers 'to promote the production of milk and ward off post-natal depression.'

In Morocco and Egypt, it isn't only the colour and material but the use of specific *patterns* to counter evil forces or that are associated with benevolent ones.

You could extrapolate the main *concepts* from blurbs such as these as the basis for activities, and grade the language according to your target group. While *longevity* is a sophisticated and less-common word, there's a lot of mileage in a discussion on things that help you live longer.

For beginners, you could create resources with patterns or colours to elicit personal responses from learners. Include discussion questions that encourage teachers to look at the jewellery worn by their own learners, such as bangles, and use that as a springboard for class discussions at any level.

Post-natal depression is a relevant topic for many ESOL learners, who we have seen are very often mothers in difficult circumstances. This is an innovative and safe way of introducing a sensitive subject, and promoting cross-cultural discussion that people can feel safe contributing to, without personalising it.

Representation of animals
Think of cats, fish and birds and the ideas they symbolise around the world. Snakes appear in a lot of different cultures. (With thanks again to the Iroko Theatre Company for the inspiration here.) There is the snake goddess Manasa, worshipped by Hindus in India and Bengal to

protect them from disease. In another gallery at the British Museum there is an image of a mask of the Mami Wata spirit from West Africa. Again, snakes are tied up with ideas of protection and healing. You'll also find rings from the ancient Roman era with snakes heads on as a lot of women in ancient Rome wore rings to keep them free from harm. Therefore, we can see that snakes from very different parts of the world and from different eras share commonalities and have connotations of female, protection and healing. This is an example of how we can write materials to facilitate the search for commonalities in our classrooms and for connections between learners and the new communities they are settling in.

Not only are these themes that students can *relate* to and have an opinion about, but they are topics that will generate useful lexical sets that can be transferred to and used in everyday settings. It's vocabulary that you'll find in the UK government Department for Education and Skills (DfES) *Skills for Life* materials, but presented and practised in a way that blurs traditional ways of categorising learning into 'survival English', etc. You have colours, clothing, parts of the body, furniture, materials and numbers – and not a doctor's surgery or train station in sight!

Recommended Resources

Migration museum project: *migrationmuseum.org/education/*

Geffrye Museum ESOL resources: *geffrye-museum.org.uk/learning/online-resources/esol-resources*

Victoria and Albert Museum programmes for ESOL students: *vam.ac.uk/content/articles/p/programmes-for-esol-students/*

The British Museum ESOL programmes: *britishmuseum.org/learning/adults_and_students/esol_programmes.aspx*

An inspiring exhibition about asylum that I saw at the Brighton Fringe festival a few years ago: *housefestival.org/house-artist-rosanna-martin-and-ester-svensson*

Writing Materials For Voluntary One-To-One ESOL Provision

OVERVIEW OF VOLUNTARY ESOL

ESOL is also taught by volunteers, in a range of settings across the UK, including libraries, churches and through Home Learning schemes. The voluntary sector is an important provider of ESOL classes and outreach work in the community, especially for those learners who experience difficulties in accessing formal provision or who have complex needs.

The background of those volunteering is as diverse as the learners. For example, there is the Swansea Bay Asylum Seekers Support Group, a community group formed and run on a voluntary basis by asylum seekers, refugees and local people, who run informal drop-in sessions for language support. In Bristol there are timetabled ESOL classes for refugees at the Malcolm X Centre in St Pauls, run by qualified teachers. Another example is Talk English (talk-english.co.uk), a project run by the Manchester Adult Education Service, and one of the winners of the 2015 ELTons who describe their work on their website as: '… working with people with low levels of English to help them improve their language skills, access services and get more involved in the community.' Around 3,500 learners have been beneficiaries of the project to date that is run by over 650 volunteers.

One successful home learning scheme is the Merton Home Tutoring Service (MHTS) in London. I (KAM) interviewed Sophie Johnstone (SJ), home tutoring programme coordinator, to learn more about the characteristics of *one-to-one* ESOL, with a view to understanding what kinds of materials work well in this setting and to hear about what informed their own process of materials development for this specialised field of ESOL.

(Thanks too to the tutors at MHTS, in particular Elizabeth Kennedy, Sheila Stirrat and Ruth Dawson for their ideas and suggestions that they shared with Sophie prior to the interview.)

Task 10

If you were carrying out research, in order to write materials to support voluntary one-to-one ESOL provision, consider the kinds of questions you'd need to ask.

Make a list and see if any of your questions appear in the interview below.

THE TEACHING AND LEARNING CONTEXT

KAM Could you give me an overview of the settings in which the ESOL sessions take place and some of the reasons why learners are taught one-to-one in their own homes and not in formal classes?

SJ The service is for adults in Merton who want to learn English but cannot get to college classes. There are many different reasons for this: they may have a disability or be caring for someone with a disability; they might have young children or no childcare, or nursery times clash with college class times. They might not have been to school in their own country and lack the confidence to start at college. Or they might not be able to travel or pay for a course, or they work shifts that are not compatible with college timetables. We work with several Asian women's refuges and the victims of domestic violence, who may have low confidence and not feel ready for learning in a college environment.

I assess the learner in their home and advise them onto a college course if it is appropriate. If not, then one of our volunteers works with them for an hour a week in a 1–1 capacity for six months. After this we move the learner onto a mainstream course or one of our Stepping Stones classes (a community ESOL class) or another appropriate next step. We encourage learners to participate in other community activities like going to the library, a local coffee morning, playgroup, etc.

Tutors are working in learners' own homes, and this gives rise to conversations often based on food and cooking. These are really useful, because informal conversations outside the home with neighbours are usually about things like this. It makes for authentic communication with tutors as they share ideas about cooking and things.

Learners often need a bit of help to understand letters from school, hospitals and about housing issues, for example, and these can be used to expand vocabulary of real importance to learners, things that can cause such stress if you don't understand them. Tutors can ask about wedding photos up on the walls or religious pictures that are on display or children's games to start conversations that are meaningful to the learner.

CONSIDERATIONS FOR WRITING MATERIALS FOR ONE-TO-ONE HOME TUTORS

KAM Writing for one-to-one ESOL sessions will probably require a different approach to materials development, which is often written with group teaching in mind or for self-study. What should a writer bear in mind?

SJ Materials need to portable, flexible and practical. Tutors are teaching in the learners' homes; they may be sitting together on the floor or working on a small coffee table, or on the edge of the learner's bed.

The tutor is only working with one learner so the lesson activities can focus on the needs of that learner. For example, say the learner wants to get a job as a lunchtime supervisor, the objectives would include practising interview questions, interview etiquette and how to do a firm handshake. Another learner might want to talk to their child's teacher about a specific issue or to develop confidence talking, listening and understanding on the phone. Materials are useful that can help tutors set up scenarios to help with tasks like these.

KAM So certain materials would work best as a template then, for tutors to be able to customise.

Are there any specific constraints that materials developers might need to take into consideration? What kind of materials/resources don't work?

SJ There may not be an internet connection or computer or laptop.

Tutors should avoid long presentations of teaching points or too much tutor talking. Be adaptable and change materials/topic if something pressing has come up in the learner's life that needs immediate attention – an imminent eviction, an illness, a meeting with the job centre etc. As the learner only has an hour of ESOL input a week, avoid giving them a long writing task that takes 45 minutes. Often learners have little contact with English outside of this lesson time, so tasks and materials that foster speaking skills are ideal.

A textbook resource aimed at young students attending college or a businessman having a meeting or students going skiing would not necessarily be relevant to a mother in her 30s with different ambitions and trying to cope with life in this country.

KAM What kind of resources work really well in one-to-one teaching?

SJ Worksheets that can be cut up and used for kinaesthetic tasks. For example, using coloured card cut up to re-order sentences and questions. Using pictures, a short video on your phone that you can look at together from the British Council website. Resources that reflect everyday life and engage their interests. One text book that is popular with tutors is *Friends, Families and Folktales* edited by M. Spiegel and H. Sunderland, as it has a relevant text, discussion questions and lots of ideas for follow up tasks (grammar points and writing exercises).

Another important thing to consider is that some learners might never have been to school and so resources at a low level that reinforce study skills are useful.

KAM What formats do your tutors prefer?

SJ Word docs that can be downloaded and adapted work well, so they can meet a learner's particular situation. PDFs of photos/images/illustration are invaluable for starting conversations.

KAM What are the teachers looking for in their materials?

SJ We have a range of tutors with a variety of teaching styles. Some tutors enjoy using games with their learners, some like a mini course for a few lessons, others like a lesson plan that can be easily adapted. Materials that are relevant to daily lives of ESOL learners are always popular.

KAM What about level?

SJ Mostly Entry level 1 and some pre-entry. There are higher level learners too (Entry 2, 3 and Level 1). We have a lot of spiky profile students who need help improving literacy skills and others who need to develop confidence and have an opportunity to practise oral skills.

MHTS Resources

KAM You've published your own readers. Tell us about your own approach to materials development. Why did you write them? Was it because you had identified a gap in the materials and that you couldn't find resources to meet your learners' needs?

SJ We set up a reader workshop – that was a team of our teachers writing collaboratively, to produce information booklets. This was because there weren't many commercial materials for adults at Entry 1 and Entry 2 that were relevant to our learners. Their interests often centre on information about living here, in the UK. We collected questions they usually ask, from tutors in the Record sheets they submit, our own experience of topics they are concerned with, and found we needed materials that fitted our learners better. We set up a writing workshop, and wrote our own readers, on topics like the education system in England and Wales, A & E, rubbish collection and so on.

KAM Writing is more and more a collaborative job now. How did you find it?

SJ It worked really well writing collaboratively. Each writer was an experienced teacher, and chose the topics they wanted to write on. Sessions were spent commenting and suggesting amendments to each other's drafts and sharing ideas. We consulted professionals, to make sure the information was correct. The process was fun, inspiring and creative, and we managed to produce quite a range of readers.

KAM How successful have the readers been?

SJ It has been well worth doing. The information is exactly what learners want. They are used for reading homework, reading together in a session, initiating discussions and increasing vocabulary and strings of speech. We have sold a few at a low price, so other groups and teachers can make use of them. We update the readers when we need to make changes, and run off a new edition. We have had appreciative feedback from ESOL teachers, learners and tutors.

There is a national organisation, NAVTE (National Association for the Voluntary Teaching of English), for groups that run projects involving volunteers teaching ESOL. We meet three times a year and share ideas and good practice. If you are interested in finding out more please email me at sophie.johnstone@mhts.org.uk

KAM Thank you so much for your time. And congratulations again on getting funding for the project to continue for another three years.

Sample pages from Merton Home Tutoring Readers are available to view on their homepage: *mhts.org.uk*

RECOMMENDED RESOURCES

Advice on using the New Internationalist Easier English Wiki resources in one-to-one teaching:
eewiki.newint.org/index.php/One-to-one_teaching

Some useful resources to prepare volunteer befrienders to work with adult ESOL third country nationals[13] who are planning to settle in the UK:
learningunlimited.co/files/Befriender_Training_Toolkit.pdf

Active Citizenship and English (ACE) project: The *Literacy for active citizenship readers* series (with stories written by volunteer befrienders/learners) which won a 2016 ELTon award for 'Innovation in learner resources'. There is a charge for the readers themselves but downloadable resources to support each reader are free to download from the website:
learningunlimited.co/resources/acereaders

Readers (E2 and above) written by former ESOL learners about their experiences in their countries and in the UK:
www.ourlivespress.co.uk

ESOL Readers: *gatehousebooks.co.uk*

---

[13] **third country national** Any person who is not a citizen of the EU.

Adapting And Creating Materials For ESOL In Prison

UNDERSTANDING THE LEARNING CONTEXT

There are 140 prisons in the UK. We have more prisons than universities. Foreign national prisoners account for over 14% of the prison population in England and Wales. (Ministry of Justice, 2015) It's impossible, however, to quantify the number of potential ESOL learners within any prison since many 'foreign nationals' in prison are native speakers of English (Nigerians or Canadians for example), and also many prisoners with ESOL needs, may hold British passports.

'Many foreign national prisoners speak no English at all and may have come straight to prison from the airport or seaport where they arrived. All they know of British life is the immigration queue and the inside of a prison.' (Lemos, 2014: 35)

'I learnt a bit of Spanish with a 70-year-old Colombian grandfather who'd hit hard times and tried to bring a suitcase full of cocaine through Heathrow. He didn't speak a word of English before jail and had learnt it all from the Cockney geezers on the wing. As a result he didn't understand basic outside world vocabulary such as 'traffic cone' or 'coat hanger', but he did talk about '"avin a bubble with his china plates".'
(Cattermole, 2015)

Attempts to quantify potential ESOL learners in prison internationally are compounded by the differing definitions of ESOL/ESL outside the UK, as well as different ways of describing prisoners not holding a passport in the country where they are detained. According to USimmigration.com, there are 55,000 foreign nationals in prison in the US (25% of the prison population), and approximately 38,500 are Mexican nationals. It also refers to this group as 'imprisoned foreign aliens'. In Australia, nearly 20% of prisoners are foreign, defined as 'being born outside Australia.' (prisonstudies.org) As discussed above, we can't rule out English-speakers from this category. However, we can surmise that in all English-speaking countries, prisoners with low levels of English or no English make up a significant, and growing, proportion of the prison population.

Task 11

Make a list of factors that create additional challenges for ESOL teaching and learning in custodial settings, above and beyond those of mainstream ESOL.

Consider:
- possible characteristics of offender-learners and the range of needs
- constraints arising from the prison setting and regime

Compare your answers with the commentary on page 83.

These will have implications for the design and content of ESOL prison resources. Therefore, you will need to research and gain a sound understanding of the learning and teaching context of the prison you are writing for. This will differ from prison to prison and country to country. You need to think about the category of prison; is it high security Category A with prisoners on long term sentences, a Category B or C prison, or a remand prison, where prisoners are in for weeks and not years? Is it male, female or a young offenders institution (YOI)? Open (Cat-D) or closed?

An insider's view: 'B-cat prisons in my experience are like a sorting office; most people don't stay there for too long before they get moved on to a different prison. In a B-cat you'll meet everyone from triple murderers waiting for extradition to bitties [addicts] doing a month for stealing a packet of sausages. ... C-cats are basically a B-cat in the middle of nowhere with less security and less staff...' (Cattermole, 2015)

ESOL PROVISION

ESOL provision will be affected by the same constraints as other areas of prison education. In the commentary you'll have seen a list of factors that lead to a highly unsettled learning environment. Learners arrive late or in waves, depending upon the availability of prison officers to escort them from the wings to class. They are constantly moved from prison to prison and they are affected by issues such as drug use, depression and anxiety. This will also be compounded by the additional challenges of teaching foreign learners who may not understand what is happening to them, be miles away from families and be having deportation hanging over their heads.

Bearing the characteristics of this particular setting in mind, materials writers will need to think about:
- Producing resources for standalone sessions that can accommodate the disrupted nature of the learning, and the roll-on, roll-off provision.
- Ensuring resources can be used for multi-level classrooms, so include differentiated tasks and learning outcomes. (Although learners with low levels of literacy or who are not literate in their own language are not

more likely to be in a prison ESOL classroom than a community one, they *are* more likely to be taught alongside learners with more proficiency in English. In some prisons there are such small numbers of ESOL learners that they are just taught as a group, regardless of level.)
- Not including texts or images that assume prior knowledge of UK culture (and not including images of babies or children in certain prisons).
- Ensuring materials have a wide variety of activities and will be able to sufficiently engage learners with short concentration spans, or who may be on methadone (e.g. avoid lots of instructions and text on the page).
- Providing a range of alternative classroom procedures should things not go according to plan (pair and group work can be political and learners may feel unsafe moving from their seats).
- Including 'soft skills' in the learning outcomes (building confidence and self-esteem; concentration skills, study skills, anger management).
- Including materials that prepare them for living and working on the outside and are aspirational, not only focussed on inside life. Football has also been mentioned as being a popular theme for classroom discussions.
- The formal qualifications that they will be working towards.
- Providing opportunities for offender-learners to develop pragmatic competence[14] in English. Indeed '… many ELT texts … continue to concentrate on the acquisition of linguistic competence, with insufficient attention to a fuller communicative competence.' (Boxer and

---

[14] **pragmatic competence** The ability to use language in a way that is appropriate for the context, and understanding how language is related to the situation in which it is used.

Pickering, 1995, cited in Harwood, 2010:10) This is critical in a prison context: 'speakers who do not use pragmatically appropriate language run the risk of appearing uncooperative at the least, or, more seriously, rude or insulting.' (ibid:10).

EXPLORING THE REAL-LIFE NEEDS OF OFFENDER-LEARNERS

Your starting point should be the same as for mainstream ESOL, i.e. thinking about the real-life needs of the learners, in this case the offender-learners. Prisons have their own culture, regime and routines, and even argot, and this will also differ from prison to prison. There also seem to be abbreviations and acronyms everywhere! They seemed to me to be a large part of prison-speak and ubiquitous on prison forms. You'll need to find out the situations when offender-learners will need to use English, for reading, writing, speaking and listening and consider the features and functions of literacy practices that are peculiar to prison settings. For example, filling in apps (prison application forms) to do most things, like see the doctor or join a gym. Some prisons have online apps, others don't. There will be different ways of ordering food and different places to collect the food. Some prisoners eat on the wings, others in dining rooms.

Nowhere more so than in prison, does the use of EFL coursebooks seem more incongruous and inappropriate. It's difficult to imagine how the learning outcomes of EFL books could be relevant to the lives and needs of offender learners. The same can be said for general ESOL materials which set out to develop learners' ability to talk to school teachers, book a doctor's appointment on the phone or buy a train ticket. So how to write content that is relevant and motivates learners because they know it's the kind of language they need in order to get by in this environment, and once they are released?

Task 12

Make a list of some situations when prisoners need to speak, listen, read and write in English, that will require context-specific language and knowledge of prison culture and regimes.

Think about the people in a prison they might need to talk to, for example, wing reps[15].

Compare your answers with the commentary on page 84.

PLANNING CONTENT

I've discussed in earlier sections how an authentic text-based (spoken and written) approach to materials development is important in achieving learner-centredness in materials.

Task 13

Make a list of authentic texts that you could find in prison, to contextualise the key target vocabulary, grammar and functions that learners might need.

Compare your answers with the commentary on page 84.

These texts are an excellent way of contextualising the learning so that it's relevant. You can use them to extrapolate key vocabulary, grammar and functions and

---

[15] **wing rep (wing representative)** Prisoners voted in by other prisoners on their wing. Identified by wearing different coloured T-shirts.

they will be localised and therefore you'll be able to better personalise the learning.

It would also be good practice to embed wider social outcomes in your materials, e.g. mapped to 'The seven pathways to reducing reoffending'; pathways devised by the National Offender Management Service (NOMS). These recognize that if you help offenders deal with certain factors, they are less likely to reoffend. The key areas are:

Accommodation   Education, Training & Employment
Health   Finance, Benefit & Debt Management
Drugs & Alcohol Children and Families
Attitudes, Thinking & Behaviour

You can find more information about this online and use these topic areas as a springboard for your content planning. An example could be to create a resource that helps offenders complete a criminal conviction disclosure statement on a job application form, and map this to the Education, Training and Employment pathway. Or design an activity in which the teacher can set up a role play where this is discussed at an interview. Or you could devise a listening activity based on a prisoner enquiring about how to join an alcoholic support group, under 'Drugs and Alcohol', with a grammar focus on question forms. Offender learners need to learn about the system and procedures inside the prison (and outside on release, if they are not being deported), as well as acquiring the language.

So, to conclude, I'll bring you back to my first statistic regarding the number of prisons in relation to the number of universities. Consider the wealth of materials related to EAP (English for Academic Purposes). Just imagine the social return if we invested even a fraction of this in developing resources suitable for ESOL in prison.

Writing Digital Content For Low-Level ESOL Learners

An online survey conducted by the British Council in June 2013 revealed that most learners using its online resources were studying at Entry 3[16]/Level 1. Across the board there were very few online resources for beginners. The ESOL Nexus project, co-funded by the European Integration Fund[17] supporting the integration of third country nationals, set out to address this need. (The project terminated at the end of June 2015 although the resources are still freely available for download.) The resources have proven to be extremely successful and popular. You may want to create your own content customised to the needs of your learners or to write for other platforms that serve the needs of ESOL learners (see the Commentary for Task 4 on page 78 for a list of websites).

This section will look at some of the issues involved in writing *interactive* online practice materials for ESOL learners. Note that not all online content is interactive. Some materials are lesson plans or worksheets that are hosted by an ESOL website and are available as downloadable PDFs. The rationale for these is i) to support busy teachers, and ii) provide resources for teachers working in low-tech community environments, or custodial settings where learners don't have access to the open Internet. You may want to create online resources for the

---

[16] **Entry 3** One of the national standards of English language proficiency as defined by the Adult ESOL Core Curriculum. It is roughly aligned with the CEFR level B1. At this level, ESOL learners' spoken competence is often much better than their literacy skills.

[17] **European Integration Fund** The EIF promotes EU member states work in integrating third country nationals.

closed prison intranet called Virtual Campus but be prepared to wait over a year for it to get past the vetting procedures before it goes live.

Before you begin, it's important to remember that interactive online activities need to be underpinned by the same robust pedagogy as those you write for the classroom. You then need to find creative ways to fit the technology to your learning outcomes. If you take the technology as your starting point, you're unlikely to achieve any flow in your design, progression or real learning. Just as a pen won't produce a novel on its own, a fancy authoring package won't produce a learning tool without your ESOL expertise. (For further reading on using authoring tools and for an overview of the different task types available, see the ELT Teacher 2 Writer ebook, *How to Write for Digital Media*).

When I receive a brief to write digital content to support mainstream EFL course books, there is an underlying assumption that the market is digitally savvy and that the students will know how to navigate the learning objects and understand the metalanguage[18] of the online environment.

Task 14

Think of some unique challenges that may arise when creating digital content for ESOL learners, as opposed to EFL learners. Consider lower level or beginner learners in particular.

Compare your answers with the commentary on page 85.

---

[18] **metalanguage** Language used to describe language or linguistic features. It's the language teachers use to talk about the English language, teaching and learning, e.g. *auxiliary verb*.

Therefore, we have seen that you may need to consider how to prepare learners for what might be a completely new learning experience. There are likely to be issues with navigating the modules and the fact that some task types are more *intuitive* than others. Ease of use is critical for self-access. In practice this means that learners feel more at ease with online tasks that they may have met in textbooks, such as matching, as opposed to hotspots[19], which are exclusively online task types and may present a barrier to learners with emerging digital literacies.

Breaking down the barriers

If you are providing teacher's notes or procedural notes, you might want to include activities that pre-teach some of the digital jargon. If the resource is *purely* self-access, you ought to consider creating a practice module. You could have videos created by screen capture software to model the functionality of a particular task type. This could be followed by an activity where the learner can just practise manipulating the mouse, matching, dragging and dropping. If the language on-screen is well below level, this will enable users to focus on the *process* of the online activity, as opposed to getting the answers right. With beginners you might think this is difficult, but you only need to have two items on a page that are obviously different (animal, baby) and learners get to match photos and words, using the mouse to click on images or drag words across the screen. (Just as I discussed underlying pedagogy earlier – you should be guided by what works in the classroom, so in an

---

[19] **hotspot** An online task type that generally consists of an interactive image programmed to give a particular response, depending upon where exactly the user clicks on the image (e.g. *Click on the maternity ward in the hospital plan*).

authentic task, you'd be aiming for between 6–8 items and no more.)

At this stage, a lot of the learning experience is about getting learners to try out the technology, and just learning by doing and 'having a go'. These practice modules can play an important role in developing transferable digital skills, so it's worth the effort from a teaching perspective as they serve more than one purpose.

A key challenge is then how to use the technology to scaffold the experience learners have online, and guide them more in terms of navigating the resources. This is with a view to helping learners to overcome barriers to learning arising from poor computer skills. It's a case of focussing on the *opportunities* technology presents in this learning context, rather than on the constraints. In this way, building confidence and the development of digital and visual literacy become an important wider learning outcome.

Task 15

In what ways could the technology be used to scaffold the learning objects?

(Hint: Consider online features of software programmes, such as audio etc. and things you may use in a word processor when you get stuck.)

Compare your answers with the commentary on page 86.

We've seen ways to exploit i) the technology and ii) the specific features of authoring tools in order to facilitate learners' online experience. The language of the rubrics[20]

---

[20] **rubric** Instructions for a task.

needs to be at the appropriate level so that the instructions are comprehensible too. Since you want to be instructing learners in a self-access environment, these rubrics need to be clear, unambiguous and only asking the learners to do one thing at a time.

Task 16

Look at the rubrics below (a–c) and answer the questions.

1 Why could they be problematic for beginner ESOL learners?

2 Can you suggest alternatives?

a. Unscramble the letters to create adjectives.

b. Click on the image of a dentist.

c. Complete the sentences with the correct choice of verb and put them in the right order to make a paragraph.

Compare your answers with the commentary on page 87.

LEVEL OF CHALLENGE AND PROVIDING FEEDBACK

One of the main aims is to build learners' confidence, therefore the activities should be at a level that is challenging but achievable. Use feedback to boost motivation and a sense of achievement. This dynamic feedback is one of those advantageous features of the online medium over paper. Learners make a choice and corresponding feedback appears.

Normally authoring packages allow for multiple tries. If the learner selects the wrong answer, provide a tip to help the learner get to the right answer. If they don't get there, provide clear, succinct feedback about why the correct answer is correct so that if they choose to work through the module again, they'll get it next time. This is a very important learning aid, turning incorrect choices into learning opportunities: we can learn a lot from making mistakes. If you are giving a final score, avoid feedback such as *You failed*. It could be the first time a learner has ever done anything online at all.

You should also provide feedback that is like the kind of feedback a learner would get from a teacher; brief, direct and personal (use *you* for example) and avoiding metalanguage.

The amount of scaffolding you provide (in rubrics, by providing examples, pop-up windows) can affect the level of difficulty. You can also determine the level of challenge by the *type* of task you choose. Generally speaking, matching tasks (pictures and key words) are easier than other activities. It's an activity type that learners will be familiar with from games and course books. Activities such as drop down or drag and drop are intrinsically more difficult because they demand a certain amount of digital literacy and are not immediately intuitive to someone who's new to this. Finally, type in activities are the most difficult as they require the learners to produce, rather than simply select something. At beginner level I would suggest the learners are required to type in a letter or word. It will be at your discretion as a writer as to whether to penalise them on getting the correct upper or lower case. It will ultimately depend on the language focus.

CONTENT

The starting point for the focus of your online materials should be the same as for print resources. Your approach should still be informed by an understanding of the real life needs and characteristics of the learners and key language structures need to be contextualised in order to meet those specific needs. Interactive online materials offer lots of creative opportunities for the learner to be able to experience language in use and practise the language in useful ways.

Key language items can be contextualised in reading or listening texts, or in short animations presented in embedded videos. Activities should provide opportunities for learners to notice language features. Tasks should become progressively more challenging and activate target vocabulary. Comprehension questions on video content should include questions that are also intended to develop learners' visual literacy. (You become a better language learner when you increase your visual skills because you are taking cues from the environment.) Lower level learners can learn at their own pace, pausing and replaying the video or audio files.

Writing modules should lead to some type of language output (writing a very short text message for stronger learners, filling in a form) and where possible create the opportunity for the learners to respond to the content on a personal level. Of course, in many online learning environments it's impossible to assess this type of 'free writing' activity automatically (although progress is being made in this area) – but evidence from feedback (from piloters using the ESOL Nexus online activities) found that learners still completed the tasks and found them engaging.

You can still provide a model answer that appears after they have typed their answer so that they can compare it.

You can also see if the authoring package has the functionality that allows the learner to print off what they have typed or if they are able to submit it to a teacher. If you need to include feedback or assessment on writing skills, you'll need to design activities to practise *sub-skills* such as sequencing connectives using a drag and drop gap-fill, or categorising informal and formal language.

For online spelling activities it is important to incorporate strategies that focus on visual memory. Use colours for particular word strings, cut words into chunks and move the parts around, find smaller words within longer words.

Other features that are available are glossaries. You can have cultural glossaries to deal with dialectical variations.

It's good practice to include a final step that encourages learners to reflect on their learning and self-evaluate according to the learning objectives of the module. This information can be printed off and transferred to ILPs/ provide the basis for a record of learning.

All in all, if done well, online learning for beginners can provide an engaging, visual and kinaesthetic learning experience.

Embedding Equality And Diversity In ESOL Materials

The issue of equality and diversity is vast and would merit an ebook in itself. The aim of this section is to provide a starting point for you to *reflect* on what it means to create inclusive materials, that can truly foster equality and celebrate diversity.

ESOL writers are not as constrained by market forces as some EFL writers and publishers. That's what makes writing ESOL materials so exciting. It's also where you are likely to already find materials that are more representative of the super-diverse groups of learners we teach in the UK.

In mainstream ELT publishing you'll come across the acronym PARSNIPs; a shorthand for the things writers are told to avoid in their materials. It's essentially self-censorship, but if you want your book to sell, you'll probably need to adhere to it. PARSNIPs stands for **p**olitics, **a**lcohol, **r**eligion, **s**ex, **n**arcotics, -**i**sms and **p**ork.

As ESOL practitioners, we are striving to create or adapt materials so that they address real-life needs and are meaningful to learners. Ideally resources will lead to wider learning outcomes. Some of the issues that are deemed off-limits in EFL contexts would be unavoidable in a prison ESOL context, for example. If you are hoping to create a resource that equips offender-learners with the language to access drug or alcohol rehabilitation programmes you'll need to make sure the target vocabulary includes alcohol and drugs.

Furthermore, the problem with PARSNIPs-type rule books is that they can be used to justify the omission of pretty much any issue that is not deemed to be 'safe' as we'll see below.

While I was researching this ebook, I came across the following ELT publication: '*Taboos and Issues: Photocopiable Lessons on Controversial Topics*' by Richard MacAndrew and Ron Martinez (2001). The blurb says:

'*Taboos and Issues* is the latest in the series of photocopiable Teachers' Resource Books. It covers many serious issues which are usually, *and quite reasonably*, [my italics] considered unsuitable for inclusion in general coursebooks. It provides the opportunity for adults to discuss controversial issues.'

I'd like to share the contents page with you for you to reflect on.

1. Death
2. Nudity
3. Politically Incorrect Jokes
4. Taboo Conversation Topics
5. It Should Be Banned!
6. Not My Type
7. Sex for Sale
8. Swearing
9. Torture
10. Sexual Harassment
11. Bribery and Corruption
12. Designer Babies
13. Children Who Kill
14. Gays and Jobs
15. Animal Rights
16. Marriage – For Better or For Worse
17. Nobody Needs a Gun

18. The Sale of Human Organs
19. AIDS
20. Telling Lies
21. Abortion
22. National Stereotypes
23. Cheating On Your Partner
24. Are You Happy With Your Body?
25. Immigration and Racism
26. Changing Sex
27. Is This News?
28. The Right To Die
29. Old Enough To Be Her Grandfather!
30. Big Brother Is Watching
31. Anxiety and Depression

There is the implicit suggestion that to bring homosexuality or mental illness, racism or addiction into the classroom is to somehow *transgress*. By labelling something as 'taboo' or as 'an issue' the writers seem to be defining what can and can't be talked about; separating topics into those perceived as 'normal' and those that are 'not normal'. As educators (and materials writers) we need to ask the question (and encourage our learners to ask) – Who makes these distinctions? The categories that we create in language are the ones that are used in society. Therefore, by defining something as 'taboo' we are automatically separating people that identify with that category from the mainstream.

The same authors wrote another, more safely titled book: *Instant Discussions* (2003). The blurb for this:

'*Instant Discussions* is designed to bridge the gap between the classroom and real life by giving students the opportunity to talk about things which really matter to them on a personal level.'

The contents include chapter 12 *Jewellery for men,* and chapter 20 *Ever eaten dog?*

If you are working in publicly funded education in the UK, you are legally required to ensure that your teaching practice is inclusive (The Public Sector Equality Duty: *equalityhumanrights.com/en/advice-and-guidance/public-sector-equality-duty*). The Equality Act 2010 provides the legal framework for embedding equality and diversity. This section, therefore, considers how to create ESOL materials that we can describe as inclusive, not controversial.

As a starting point, let's consider *equality and diversity* in terms of the nine protected characteristics[21] that are defined in the Equality Act 2010.

Task 17

What are the nine protected characteristics?

Compare your answers with the commentary on page 88.

Classroom materials play an important role in helping to challenge discrimination. If educators perpetuate the idea, in any area of their work, that certain groups of people are distinct or any discussion is 'of a sensitive nature', then that is contrary to inclusive teaching practices. Furthermore, learners internalise the message that they are 'different'. An English student with Special Educational Needs was describing his exam concessions to me: "I get an extra 25% time. When the normal students finish their exams, I wait behind and do another half hour."

---

[21] **protected characteristics** The Equality Act 2010 introduced this term to refer to groups that are protected by the law from discrimination.

It's not simply the fact of certain identities being described as taboo or controversial, or 'potentially sensitive' that perpetuates the marginalisation of groups. The *omission* of topics and groups is also discriminatory. At the NATECLA (National Association for Teaching English and Community Languages to Adults) conference in October 2012 'Breaking the ice: addressing LGBT (Lesbian, Gay, Bisexual, Transgender) issues in the ESOL classroom', John Gray gave an inspiring presentation on the 'invisibility' of LGBT groups in EFL materials. (*englishagenda.britishcouncil.org/continuing-professional-development/teacher-educator-framework/understanding-teaching-context/breaking-ice-addressing-lgbt-issues-esol-classroom*)

Cartwright (2006) states that: '… one of the most effective and insidious ways of oppressing gay people has been to deny their existence.'

Equality and Diversity UK published a Post-16 Education Toolkit, in which they refer to 'mainstreaming'; an approach to 'embedding equality and diversity into everyday practice …'

'Equality and diversity in teaching and learning should be delivered by mainstreaming these issues into the curriculum. Equality and diversity has to be embedded into all aspects of the curriculum: from session planning and teaching methods to assessment procedures; from inclusive resources and materials to teaching which explore the nature and impact of discrimination, harassment and victimisation because of disability, race, sex, sexual orientation, transgender, religion or belief, age and so on.' (p80)

In terms of materials development, the aim should be that diversity becomes a regular and routine feature of resources. In other words, all identities and groups should eventually be considered part of mainstream classes and related issues not be labelled as 'taboo' or controversial.

'The language, resources, images and contexts used in the classroom should be inclusive and diverse – mirroring the learners' own lives and offering insight into other lives.' (ibid, p81)

Task 18

Make a list of some features of what you consider to be 'inclusive' materials.

Compare your answers with the commentary on page 89.

Inclusive materials should therefore reflect the whole community of which your learners are a part and with which they hope to integrate. ESOL materials, such as the Skills for Life packs, do reflect minority ethnic communities to a certain extent, in the photographs and names that they use. The British Council ESOL Nexus website is also a model of good practice. I would argue that positive representations of disability, the elderly and LGB and T people are largely missing from publications in general however.

Materials should also contain *activities* that promote an active engagement with issues of racism, harassment and victimisation. The toolkit suggests that content should:

- teach about groups that face discrimination, harassment and victimisation
- teach learners about personal/cultural/institutional discrimination

- explore reasons why discrimination occurs
- build learners' capacity to challenge discrimination against themselves and others
- encourage learners to stand up for themselves, each other and unknown others
- provide learners with an insight into the experience of being discriminated against, discriminating, witnessing discrimination and taking action against discrimination
- engage learners in learning activities directly related to exploring injustice, inequality, prejudice, discrimination and human rights. (ibid, p82)

Materials that are inclusive and skilfully written will support the classroom management of learners who may have different views on homosexuality or gender. Please see the list of links and recommended reading in the commentary to Task 18 on page 89 for more on this.

The list above serves as sound starting point for materials design. From this you can extrapolate the contexts, key vocabulary, grammar structures and functions learners will need in order to combat discrimination, in class and beyond.

SUMMARY

- Make sure that people with the nine protected characteristics are visible in your materials.
- Avoid and challenge stereotypical representations.
- 'Mainstream' the issues.
- Consider the headings or labels you give tasks and activities: what values are you transmitting?
- Make inclusivity as integral a part of your materials design as differentiation, not simply a bolt-on.

- Contextualise target language in content that raises awareness of issues relating to equality and diversity, including celebrating diversity.

Task 19

Now select a random worksheet or open an EFL coursebook at any place.

Can you see any reference to people with one of the nine protected characteristics?

Summary Of The Writing Process

- Identify the ESOL learning context, learners, stakeholders and the characteristics of the learning and teaching environment.
- Carry out a needs analysis of learners based on real-life communicative needs and wider learning aims.
- Do an audit of current resources to identify gaps/shortcomings.
- Research authentic texts to contextualise learning of grammar, lexis and functions.
- Explore innovative ways to exploit texts for learner-centred activities and provide opportunities for personalisation in order to promote deeper learning.
- Ensure people with the nine protected characteristics are visible in your resources in a mainstream and non-stereotypical way.
- Design tasks and activities that are underpinned by theories of second language acquisition; ensure there is a flow, clear progression and that they lead to clear learning outcomes.
- Include suggestions for differentiation for mixed-level classes.
- Include teacher's notes for your materials so they can be easily used by other teachers.
- Pitch tasks at the appropriate cognitive level for adult learners with rich life experiences.
- Evaluate your resource: are there underpinning theories that validate your approach? Will your materials really facilitate language learning and promote discussion? Are the activities learner-centred? Do you provide opportunities for learners to recycle their learning and revisit target language in new contexts?

- Reference the qualifications and credit framework in your country, such as the QCF/SQCF, so that teachers can easily find what they are looking for.
- Pilot/peer review.
- Amend and redraft according to feedback.

Commentaries On Tasks

Task 1

1   You may have thought of some of the following – but I'm sure there will be more as providers seek ever-more innovative ways of reaching learners in the face of increasing funding cuts:
FE colleges, work-based learning, adult and community learning centres, Sure-Start centres, prisons, schools, learners' homes, women's refuges, church halls, refugee welcome centres, grassroots community groups, libraries, cafés, museums
And the mode of provision is diverse too: online and face-to-face learning, formal ESOL lesson delivery, informal ESOL lesson delivery, discrete ESOL courses, ESOL embedded in vocational courses, accredited and non-accredited provision

2   refugees; asylum seekers; migrant workers; new arrivals; immigrants from settled communities who have been in the UK for many years and who may hold British passports; spouses of the aforementioned; foreign national prisoners[22] who are not native speakers of English.

Task 2

Some suggestions:
Development of interpersonal skills; social skills; building confidence in literacy, digital literacy, visual literacy; developing confidence interacting with peers or other parents; participating more fully in children's school life, helping with homework; numeracy skills; ICT skills; self-

[22] **foreign national prisoners** Term used to classify prisoners who do not have a UK passport.

esteem; personal development; health awareness; improving health outcomes; well-being

TASK 3

Some suggestions:
- superdiversity

ESOL materials should provide activities and tasks that *draw on* the superdiversity of classes.
'Learners' different cultural backgrounds and life experiences offer a natural 'information gap' which can be exploited in a multitude of ways...' (Hann et al., 2010)

Ensure that your materials portray and refer to the diverse backgrounds and life experiences (more on this in the section on Equality and Diversity).

Make sure your activities don't assume prior knowledge of the UK (include lead-in tasks, pre-reading and pre-listening activities to activate schema[23]) and materials aren't Eurocentric in the values or worldview they transmit

- mixed-level classes

While you'll be writing for one particular level (pre-entry – Level 2), be mindful of the fact that there may be learners below or above that level in the class. Some suggestions:

Avoid being over-prescriptive in lesson plans you publish – teachers need to be able to adapt to own classes – provide authorable documents or templates that can be tailored to local needs.

---

[23] **schema** Background knowledge and life experiences that shape our conceptual understanding of the world.

Suggest tips for differentiating tasks and activities; provide extension activities for early finishers or stronger learners and strategies for scaffolding tasks for pre-entry learners with differentiated worksheets.

- different lengths of stay in the UK

Materials ought not to include texts that make assumptions about learners' cultural awareness of the UK and always provide lead-in tasks that activate schema.

- complex problems of learners

Content needs to be selected sensitively and tasks designed in a way that won't make learners feel exposed or put on the spot, forced to deal with painful subjects in a space they don't consider 'safe' (for example mixed classes).

Ensure you are culturally sensitive, yet inclusive according to the Equality Act (see section on Equality and Diversity for fuller discussion).

TASK 4

1   You may have mentioned some of the following popular online ESOL resources:
- *esol.britishcouncil.org* Lesson plans, online self-access modules and a Beginners section for low-level learners.
- *esol.excellencegateway.org.uk*
- *onlinecentresnetwork.org/resources/teaching-english*
- Easier English Wiki – *New Internationalist*: PDFs and PowerPoint files of self-access and ready-made lessons with procedural notes. (Linda Ruas's *Global Justice in Easier English* workbooks were published in Nov 2016: *ethicalshop.org/global-justice-in-easier-english.html*)
- *skillsforlifenetwork.com*
- *esolscotland.com*

- *esoluk.co.uk*
- *skillsworkshop.org/esol*
- *esolcourses.com* Resources for teachers and self-access for learners.
- *onestopenglish.com/esol* Lesson plans and worksheets.
- *learningunlimited.co/resources/downloads*

Innovative English language resources produced in Australia that use song and stories to inspire intermediate to advanced learners and 'reinvigorate the classroom': *urbanlyrebirds.com*

And an example of a self-published resource to teach phonics to ESOL learners, courtesy of Nicola Dean of Rotherham College: *esol94.wixsite.com/phonics*

Many ESOL teachers also rely on resources that were not written specifically for ESOL learners. It may be that they are working in low-tech settings and are not able to use online resources that require multimedia equipment, and are perhaps using EFL coursebooks such as *English File*, *Reward* or *Cutting Edge*. Others use websites that were written for EFL teachers and students working and studying outside the UK such as these:
- *learnenglish.britishcouncil.org*
- *teachitworld.com*
- *bbc.co.uk/skillswise*

2   Some of the differences you might have mentioned include:
- the *learning* aims of the materials; those designed for use outside the UK will not be useful for preparing ESOL learners for life in the UK and citizenship;
- *ESOL* resources address wider needs and incorporate soft outcomes more often

- *EFL* resources will assume a certain educational background, and take study skills and digital literacy skills for granted.
- EFL *resources* are more 'grammar-driven'.
- Although you will find resources for beginner *learners* of English (A1), these are targeted at students who are likely to already be studying and in general are not aimed at learners with no formal educational background or who have low levels of literacy. Therefore, when designing materials, we need to be mindful of the fact that materials written for beginner EFL learners will not always be suitable for classes of beginner ESOL learners.
- Beginner resources may have been designed for children, in which case they won't be suitable for adults.
- EFL materials often pitch content at a higher *cognitive* level that makes them more intellectually engaging.
- Another difference is that if you are relying on online ESOL resources, many of these may have been *submitted* by practitioners and not gone through an editorial or quality assurance process – therefore the EFL materials, although not always relevant, can often be more desirable from that point of view.
- *Functional* language is sometimes a bolt-on in EFL materials, whereas it is often core in ESOL.
- *Illustrations* and photos may not reflect the diverse backgrounds of ESOL learners; use of professional photo libraries which tend to stock Eurocentric, white, middle-class images, and images of non-native speakers are often stereotypical.
- EFL materials often include cultural references that *assume* a certain level of knowledge of UK and western culture, so they may need to be adapted if used in an ESOL class. A prison teacher told me that one learner had no concept of what a library was. (This is also a

concern for EFL materials developers. I was recently writing a workbook for a region where nomadic tribes lived – we had to omit references to lifts.).
- EFL resources are often more professionally *produced* and glossy, with ESOL materials spiral bound and photocopied.

TASK 6

Some suggestions:
- Selecting food for the week from a school menu
- Text message about not having nuts in lunchboxes because of allergies
- NHS guidelines for picky/fussy eaters
- Selecting food options from a party invitation

All of the above would generate inter-cultural discussion in the classroom and provide lots of opportunities for personalising the learning.

TASK 7

Suggestions for possible activities:
1 Activities could fall into three categories:
i) discussion activities to activate learners schemata related to museums and to get them thinking about the role of museums and of past experiences of museums/pre-conceptions, ii) tasks which are used to pre-teach key vocabulary (e.g. labelling, matching, categorising activities) and concepts in order to make the visit the more meaningful; target structures and functions, e.g. for expressing an opinion, comparing and contrasting and then iii) documents related to planning the visit (and follow-up visits), e.g. maps, bus timetables, museum leaflets, etc.

2   Learner trails: activities which get learners exploring the galleries and paintings, searching for objects, for characters in paintings; spaces to record connections they make between objects (not just perceived meanings but shapes and materials too). A space for learners to record their personal responses (these could be tables or speech bubbles from characters on display); to notice the arrangement of objects in portraits; info gap activities to stretch learners to describe scenes in pictures or objects for partners to find.

3   Suggest activities that link in with online fine art resources; cues and prompts for follow-up class discussions; provide exemplar forms to prepare for authentic tasks such as joining the museum mailing list to be informed about future events. You could also use texts generated by the Language Experience approach for emerging readers and build up a bank of these. Follow the link for online CPD training for teachers on this approach here: *esol.britishcouncil.org/content/teachers/staff-room/continuing-professional-development/language-experience*.

See also Janet Isserlis's questionnaire responses in Appendix 2 (page 108) in which she describes a Language Experience approach to materials development.

TASK 8

Here are some suggestions and you may have come up with many of your own:
happiness, family, power, status, education, home, celebration, motherhood, protection, wealth.

You will need to grade the level of the words according to the group you are writing for, but we're asking learners to bring their own meanings and interpretations to these concepts based upon the objects that resonate for them – there are no right or wrong answers. If you produce the worksheets in a Word document, then teachers can adapt these to meet the needs of their groups as appropriate.

TASK 9

Some of the things you may have thought of: rings, shoes, writing/drawing instruments, drinking vessels ... all of these objects lend themselves to the framework I used for materials based on the theme of chairs.

TASK 11

Some characteristics to bear in mind:
- Spiky profile brings a whole new meaning in this context. Multi-level classes are the norm and backgrounds vary enormously in all respects.
- Some ESOL learners will be UK nationals, others will be non-nationals; some will be awaiting 'removal' and others will be returning to the community in the UK. Others will have actually served their sentence, but are waiting in prison for deportation. Some offender learners will have lived in the UK, while others may have come straight from the airport.
- Entry 1 is perhaps the most prevalent level with significant numbers of pre-entry learners in classes.
- poor study skills
- low attention spans
- learners withdrawing from drugs or on methadone
- prevalence of mental illness
- in-class tensions spilling over from the wings

Some constraints:
- frequent turnover with prisoners being moved from one prison to another (this is known as being 'ghosted' when it's unexpected)
- disrupted starts to classes with learners arriving in dribs and drabs
- constraints regarding the format of resources and access to online materials

TASK 12

Some suggestions:
Speaking and listening
- asking for prison services e.g. drugs, sexual health
- talking to officers
- agreeing/disagreeing
- listening to announcements on the tannoy system
- listening to prison radio

Writing
Completing apps for a visit, phone PIN, library, gym

Reading
Posters, health information leaflets, canteen sheet, prison menus, course information

TASK 13

Some ideas:
- canteen sheets (selection of items prisoners can buy with prison earnings)
- official documents
- legal letters
- Comp 1 forms (formal complaint forms)
- property hand out applications

- VO (Visiting Order) forms
- health information / leaflets / posters
- signs for different areas around the prison
- menu sheets
- course information
- *Inside Time* (*insidetime.org* – national newspaper for prisoners)

It's envisaged that people wanting to create materials for this sector will be practising prison tutors, or have contacts inside. It is not straightforward (or legal in some instances) to take documents out of a prison. You'll need to contact the Prison Governor in the first instance (available on prison webpages) who will put you in contact with the head of security to follow up your requests. A solution is to get sight of authentic texts and then to create mock-ups of the real thing. The most important thing is that your text looks authentic.

TASK 14

Here are some ideas based upon experience of writing and editing online ELT materials (and comparing the process and briefs for EFL and ESOL); reading and acting on feedback from learners and teachers; feedback from my NATECLA workshop on 'getting lower level learners online', and of course my experience as an ESOL teacher. Given the range of ESOL settings, I'm sure you'll think of others.

- Many beginner ESOL learners do not have digital literacy and are lacking in computer skills. One teacher told me how empowering her class had been with one group of learners who tried out some of the ESOL Nexus Beginners' modules and for whom it had been the first time using a mouse.

- Even before the online learning has begun there are issues with getting login usernames; knowing how to log in, remembering user names and passwords ...
- Not knowing how to navigate an online module.
- Not understanding the metalanguage of the digital environment (e.g. *double click*, *swipe*, *drag*).

TASK 15

Some suggestions:
- use of screen capture software to produce videos modelling the functionality of an activity
- use of an audio button that allows the learner to listen to the instructions. (If there is the software option to have the audio play automatically, consider the advantages of having an on-screen button: more confident learners can choose to simply read the instructions, less able learners can play the instructions as many times as they need.)
- comprehension questions for embedded videos: so that the questions are testing the language and not just memory, add mini-clips (edited extracts featuring the relevant language input) next to the questions. This enables the learner to review the video without having to navigate away from the task.
- use a coloured background behind each text to delimit the activity so that it's clearly structured and to meet the needs of learners who are dyslexic or who encounter visual stress and need coloured overlays
- can click on gap for letters to appear one by one
- use simple icons and have audio support
- choose a sans serif font like Arial or Verdana (computer monitors have lower resolutions than printed pages and this makes small serif characters harder to read with their more complex shapes)

- consider providing scripts with video content in case they find it hard to listen to or they are using a computer without speakers or headphones
- option of a timer for stronger learners and to add an element of challenge

TASK 16

First, once you have written your clear rubric, it is good practice to provide an example. If possible, include a Help feature to play a screen capture video demonstrating the task type being carried out. And finally, if possible allow learners to be able to play an audio file so that they can hear the instruction being read out.

a. Unscramble the letters to create adjectives.
The word *unscramble* is above level and very low frequency and the learners are unlikely to know it. The verb *create* is also above level and there are easier synonyms. Learners may possibly not yet know metalanguage such as *adjectives*.
Suggested alternative: Make a word with the letters.

b. Click on the image of a dentist.
The word *click* is problematic, first because it's low-frequency if you're a digital novice and secondly because many applications are touchscreen now.
Suggested alternative: Choose the picture of a dentist.
According to the British Council's Word Family Framework of General English (*teachingenglish.org.uk/article/word-family-framework*), the word *picture* is ranked at A1 on the CEFR and the word *image* is ranked at B2, so beginner learners are more likely to understand *picture*.

c. Complete the sentences with the correct choice of verb and put them in the right order to make a paragraph.

This is too long and there is too much going on here. Make sure that you only have one instruction in one simple sentence. It's especially important to avoid complex sentences at this level. It would be better to break this down into two tasks on two separate screens. You could also scaffold the activity further by specifying the verb tense (and further by showing how it's formed).

It's not only the instructions you give learners for completing the tasks, but sometimes the default language of instructions found in authoring packages can also be quite obscure and demand a high level of digital literacy. You'll need to make sure you amend this too. For example, in some authoring packages, the default instruction is to *select a placeholder*. This could be reworded to: *choose a word*.

TASK 17

age
disability
gender reassignment (transitioning from one gender to another)
marriage and civil partnership (including same-sex couples)
pregnancy and maternity
race
religion, belief and non-belief
sex
sexual orientation

Task 18

Some suggestions, but I'm sure you'll think of many more:
- Use of case studies to build empathy
- Tasks and texts that promote cross-cultural understanding; avoidance of stereotypes (nuclear families; able-bodied athletes; heterosexual role models)
- Having photographs representing diversity of the community
- Development of reading and listening skills in the context of reading and listening about issues related to mental health, age discrimination, gay rights, etc. (For example, in the British Council ESOL Offender Learning resources, one of the listening activities is based on a prisoner discussing symptoms of depression with a prison doctor – there is still a huge stigma attached to mental health, especially amongst male prisoners.)
- Inclusion of events like Pride
- Texts containing characters with protected characteristics, but where those characteristics are not the focus of the learning activity; they have been 'mainstreamed'.

For further inspiration go to the following links where you can find model resources or authentic sources of information or texts to base your materials on:
stonewall.org.uk/at_school/links/default.asp
lgbthistorymonth.org.uk/category/schools/schools-resources/
niace.org.uk/projects/esolcitizenship/Home-Eng.htm
ukdhm.org
worldofinclusion.com/resources/#general-inclusive-education
rethink.org
vam.ac.uk/page/l/lgbtq-histories-in-the-v-and-a

Further reading
El-Metoui, L. (2014) Breaking the ice ... a closer look at lesbian, gay, bisexual and transgender lives and issues in English teaching classrooms. *Language Issues* 25/2

Cartright (2006) Mind the Gap. *Language Issues* 18/2

References

Action for ESOL (2011) ESOL News, Issue 1, September 2011.

Aldridge-Morris, K. (2005) *The Stuff of Life: ESOL Entry 3 and Level 1*. Bristol: Bristol's Museums, Galleries and Archives.

Aldridge-Morris, K. (2014) *Getting Low Level Learners Online*. NATECLA News Summer 2014 NO 105.

Baynham, M., Roberts, C., Cooke, M., Simpson S., Ananiadou, K., Callaghan, J., McGoldrick, J., and Wallace, C. (2007) *Effective teaching and learning: ESOL*. London: NRDC.

British Council (2014) Breaking the ice: addressing LGBT issues in the ESOL classroom. Available from: *http://englishagenda.britishcouncil.org/seminars/breaking-ice-addressing-lgbt-issues-esol-classroom* [Accessed 25 November 2014].

Bryers, D., Winstanley, B., Cooke, M. (2014) *The Power of Discussion*. In Mallows, D. (ed.) *Language Issues in Migration and Integration*. London: British Council.

Cartwright, A. (2006) Mind the gap, Language Issues 18/2, Autumn/Winter 2006.

Cattermole, C. (2015) *HMP – A Survival Guide*. London: Ditto Press.

Cooke, M. and Roberts, C. (2007) ESOL: Developing adult teaching and learning: Practioner Guides. NIACE.

Department for Education and Skills (DfES) (2001) *Adult ESOL Core Curriculum*. London: Basic Skills Agency/DfES.

Department for Education and Skills (DfES) (2001) Delivering Skills for Life: the national strategy for improving adult literacy and numeracy skills. London: Basic Skills Agency/DfES.

Equality and Diversity UK (2011) Embedding equality and diversity into everyday practice. Available from: *equalityanddiversity.co.uk/samples/sample-embedding-equality-and-diversity-into-everyday-practice.pdf* [Accessed 15 December 2014].

ESL Focus (2009) Teaching ESOL in America. Available from: *eslfocus.com/articles/teaching_esol_in_america-381.html* [Accessed 2 June 2015].

Hann, N. et al. (2010) ESOL Materials; Practice and Principles. In Mishan, F. and Chamber, A. (eds.) *Perspectives on Language Learning Materials Development*. Bern: Peter Lang.

Harwood, N. (2010) *English Language Teaching Materials*. Cambridge: Cambridge University Press.

International Centre for Prison Studies (2015) World Prison Brief: Australia. Available from: *prisonstudies.org/country/australia* [Accessed 1 July 2015].

Lemos, G.(2014) *The Good Prison*. London: Lemos and Crane.

NIACE (2006) More Than A Language – NIACE Committee of Inquiry on English for Speakers of Other Languages. Leicester: NIACE.

Paget, A. and Stevenson, N. (2014) On Speaking Terms: Making ESOL Policy Work Better for Migrants and Wider Society. London: DEMOS.

Roberts, C. and Cooke, M. (2009) Authenticity in the Adult ESOL Classroom and Beyond. *TESOL Quarterly* Vol 43 No.3.

Simpson, J. and Cooke, M. (2015) Teaching culture in adult ESOL in the UK. In J. Liontas (ed.) *TESOL Encyclopedia of English Language Teaching*. Malden MA: Wiley.

Tomlinson, B. (2010) *Principles of Effective Materials Development*. In Harwood, N. (ed.) English Language Teaching Materials. Cambridge: Cambridge University Press.

Tomlinson, B. (2011) Introduction: principles and procedures of materials development, in Tomlinson, B. (ed.) *Materials Development in Language Teaching* (2nd edn). Cambridge: Cambridge University Press.

Tomlinson, B. (2013) *Developing Materials for Language Teaching*. London: Bloomsbury.

US Immigration (2011) Foreign National Prison Population on the Rise: Report. Available from: *usimmigration.com/foreign-national-prison.html* [Accessed 10 May 2015].

UK Ministry of Justice (2013) Foreign national prisoners. Available from: *justice.gov.uk/offenders/types-of-offender/foreign* [Accessed 10 May 2015].

Van Patten, B. and Williams, J. (eds) 2007. *Theories in Second Language Acquisition: An Introduction.* Mahwah, NJ: Lawrence Erlbaum.

Vertovec, S (2006). The emergence of super-diversity in Britain. Working Paper No 25. Centre on Migration, Policy and Society, University of Oxford.

Appendix 1

ESL LESSON PLAN FOR NEWCOMERS TO ONTARIO

DIABETES: REDUCING THE RISK

Introduction
Diabetes: Reducing the Risk contains two units that have been designed to teach newcomers to Ontario in Adult ESL and LINC classes about diabetes and how to reduce the risks. An interdisciplinary approach has been taken to develop the units using the expertise of an ESL educator, a public health nurse, peer health educators, a Certified Diabetes Educator and a Community Food Advisor. This project is supported by the Women's Health Educator Program and Chronic Disease Prevention Program, City of Hamilton Public Health Services.

This project was initially piloted in Hamilton, Ontario in 2012. Hamilton has a large immigrant population of approximately 23.5%, with the largest percentage, 14.3%, comprised of South Asians, Blacks, and Chinese which are high-risk populations for type 2 diabetes (Statistics Canada, 2011). At that time, there were approximately 1,000 ESL/LINC (Language Instruction for Newcomers to Canada) students in Hamilton who could benefit from this material (YMCA Assessment Centre, 2012).

Questions regarding *Diabetes: Reducing the Risk*, can be sent to: Patrice Palmer, M. Ed., M.A. at palmer.patrice@gmail.com.

Curriculum
Unit 1 – What is Diabetes?
Unit 2 – Healthy Eating

Rationale
- Type 2 diabetes (T2DM) is a global epidemic, with cases rising in Canada. The total population with diabetes is projected to rise to 4.2 million (10.8%) by 2020 in Canada (Canadian Diabetes Association, 2011).
- Currently, one in four Canadians lives with diabetes, undiagnosed diabetes, or prediabetes which could rise to one in three by 2020 if this current trend continues Canadian Diabetes Association, 2011).
- Weight loss, regular physical activity, and diet have been shown to be effective methods in prevention or delay of T2DM (Ahmad and Crandall, 2010; CDA, 2011).
- Immigrants from South Asia, Latin America, the Caribbean, and sub-Saharan Africa have a two to three times greater risk of developing diabetes than Western European or North American immigrant populations (Creatore, Moineddin, and Booth, 2010).
- Typically cases of T2DM are diagnosed in adults; however there has also been a steady rise in Canada among children and youth with an over representation of South East Asians and African Canadians (Public Health Agency of Canada, 2011).
- Research suggests that immigrants arrive in Canada healthier than the average Canadian, (known as 'the healthy immigrant effect'), however within a short period of time (five to seven years); their health declines (De Maio and Kemp, 2010).

Why LINC Classrooms?
LINC (Language Instruction for Newcomers to Canada) uses a theme-based curriculum that includes topics such as health and safety, social issues, neighbourhood services, eating habits, and community resources (Center for Education and Training, 2011). *Diabetes – Reducing the*

Risks could be taught in a LINC classroom using some these themes.

'The ESL classroom provides an environment with motivated learners who are interested in improving their skills and knowledge and can use the health information in their daily lives' (Taylor et al, 2008, p380). Research by Handley, Santos, and McClelland (2009) supports the use of the ESL classroom as a site for health literacy and language learning. 'Many learners view their ESL programs as trusted sources of advice and support ... including health' (Handley et al., 2009, p54). The ESL classroom provides a nonclinical environment for dialogue for immigrants, who may become change agents in their respective communities (Handley et al., 2009).

Additional Resources
Learning About Diabetes: *learningaboutdiabetes.org*
Low literacy diabetes materials
Culturally-sensitive programs in Spanish
Canadian Diabetes Association: *diabetesgps.ca*
The Diabetes GPS is an interactive microsite developed with funding from the Public Health Agency of Canada to help people with diabetes including those from the Chinese, South Asian and African Caribbean communities access credible, culturally appropriate, and multilingual information.

Walk into Health, A Lesson Plan for ESL Instructors (*toronto.ca/City Of Toronto/Toronto Public Health/Chronic Disease and Injury Prevention/Physical Activity/File/PDF/walkintohealth_booklet.pdf*)
Toronto Public Health

Stand Up to Diabetes, Government of Ontario:
health.gov.on.ca/en/public/programs/diabetes/channel.aspx

© Patrice Palmer

References

Ahmad, L., and Crandall, J. (2010). Type 2 diabetes prevention: A review. *Clinical Diabetes, 28*(2), 53–59.

Canadian Diabetes Association. (2011). Diabetes: Canada at the tipping point. Charting a new path. Retrieved from *diabetes.ca/CDA/media/documents/publications-and-newsletters/advocacy-reports/canada-at-the-tipping-point-english.pdf*

Centre for Education and Training. (2011). Theme-based resources for LINC/ESL Classroom. Language Assessment Centres and Training Providers Services. Retrieved from *lincpeelhalton.com/LINC-Teaching-Resources/Documents/ResourcesByLINCThemes_Rev2011.pdf*

Creatore, M., Moineddin. R., and Booth. G. (2010). Age and sex-related prevalence of diabetes mellitus among immigrants to Ontario, Canada. *CMAJ, 182*(8), 781–789.

De Maio, F. G., and Kemp, E. (2010). The deterioration of health status among immigrants to Canada. Global Public Health. *5*(5):462-78

Handley, M. A., Santos, M. G., and McClelland, J. (2009). Reports from the field: Engaging learners as interpreters for developing health messages – designing the "familias Sin Plomo" English as a Second Language curriculum project. *Global Health Promotion, 16*(3), 53–58.

Public Health Agency of Canada. (2011). Diabetes in Canada: Facts and figures from a public health perspective. Retrieved from *phac-aspc.gc.ca/cd-mc/publications/diabetes-diabete/facts-figures-faits-chiffres-2011/chap4-eng.php*

Statistics Canada. (2011). National household survey (NHS). NHS focus on geography series – Hamilton, Hamilton, CMA. Immigration and ethnocultural diversity. Immigrant population. Retrieved from *www12.statcan.gc.ca/nhs-enm/2011/as-sa/fogs-spg/Pages/FOG.cfm?lang=E&level=3&GeoCode=537*)

Taylor, V. M., Cripe, S. M., Acorda, E., The, C., Coronado, G., Do, H., ... Hisplop, T. G. (2008). Development of an ESL curriculum to educate Chinese immigrants about physical activity. *J Immigrant Minority Health, 10,* 379–387.

Diabetes – Reducing the Risk: What is diabetes?

TEACHER'S NOTES AND ANSWER KEY

(CLB 4)

This lesson plan is designed to teach newcomers to Ontario in Adult ESL and LINC classes about diabetes and how to reduce the risk.   Time: approximately 2 hours

Context Outcomes
Understand the types of diabetes and how a person can reduce the risk of developing type 2 diabetes.

CLB Outcomes
Reading
- Gets the gist, key information and identified specific important detail of a two-to-three paragraph excerpt
- Compares facts and information to make choices

Writing
- Copies text with no major omissions and only occasional copying mistakes
- Follows standard conventions for capitalization and punctuation

Listening
- Elicits or provides details as needed
- Identifies specific factual details and some implied meaning

Speaking
- Asks and answers simple, factual questions

- Uses non-verbal communication (such as eye contact and nodding) to show interest and encourage conversation

ANSWER KEY

You may wish to use this quiz to determine students' knowledge about diabetes before you begin this unit.

Pre/Post Test Questions
1. There are different types of diabetes. **TRUE**
2. Diabetes is serious disease. **TRUE**
3. Only old people get type 2 diabetes. **FALSE**
4. Type 2 diabetes is increasing in Canada and around the world. **TRUE**
5. Some ethnic groups are at high risk of developing diabetes. **TRUE**
6. People who are overweight are at high risk of developing diabetes. **TRUE**

Part 2: Vocabulary Review
Pronunciation Practice
Write the following words on the board. Focus on pronunciation and syllable stress. Have students repeat after you.

're-duce	'hor-mone	'glu-cose	di-a-'be-tes
'in-su-lin	'ser-i-ous	'eth-nic	

Part 3
B. Matching Activity. Match the words with the correct definitions.
1. reduce / e. make less
2. hormone / f. a chemical in the body that travels to other parts of the body where it helps control how cells and organs work

© Patrice Palmer

3. risk / g. possibility or chance of danger, loss or injury
4. glucose / b. the main type of sugar in the blood
5. insulin / c. a hormone produced in the body to control the amount of sugar in the blood
6. serious / d. important because of possible danger
7. ethnic / a. related to race or culture

C. Cloze Activity. Fill in the blanks with the words from B.
1. Lina met other students her class from the same **ethnic** group.
2. Roberto would like to **reduce** his weight so he walks to school every day.
3. Don't run across the street. There is a **risk** that you could get hit by a car.
4. Another word for sugar in our blood is called **glucose**.
5. Driving a car without a license is **serious** problem.
6. **Insulin** controls the amount of sugar in your blood.
7. We have many **hormones** that help the cells in our bodies.

D. Ordering Activity. Put these sentences into the correct order.
4. Glucose travels in the blood to give our bodies energy.
2. Our bodies change food into glucose.
3. The hormone called insulin moves glucose through our bodies.
1. We eat food.

Part 4: Types of Diabetes
B: Reading Comprehension. Answer the questions based on Passage 2. Then check your answers with a partner.
1. What type of diabetes can occur during pregnancy? gestational diabetes
2. What type of diabetes can occur if you are a young child? type 1 diabetes
3. What keeps your blood sugar in normal? Insulin

Diabetes – Reducing the Risk: What is diabetes?

STUDENT'S WORKSHEET

Part 1: Introduction
Discuss these questions.
1. What is diabetes?
2. What is the name for diabetes in your language?
3. Do many people have diabetes in your country?
4. Why do you think some people develop/get diabetes?

Pre-test
1. There are different types of diabetes.   TRUE / FALSE
2. Diabetes is serious.   TRUE / FALSE
3. Only old people get type 2 diabetes.   TRUE / FALSE
4. Type 2 diabetes is increasing in Canada and around the world.   TRUE / FALSE
5. Some ethnic groups are at high risk for developing diabetes.   TRUE / FALSE
6. People who are overweight are at high risk of developing diabetes.   TRUE / FALSE

Part 2: Vocabulary Review
Pronunciation Practice
're-duce
'hor-mone
'glu-cose
di-a-'be-tes
'in-su-lin
'ser-i-ous
'eth-nic

© Patrice Palmer

Part 3: Reading
A. Read Passage 1.

Diabetes
Your body changes the food you eat into sugar. This sugar is called glucose. Glucose travels in your blood to all the cells in your body. The cells need glucose for energy. Insulin is a hormone that helps glucose move from your blood into your cells. Without insulin, your cells can't get the glucose (sugar) it needs.
You have diabetes when you don't have enough insulin to move glucose (sugar) from the blood into cells, or when your body doesn't use insulin properly. Diabetes means you have too much sugar in your blood.
No one knows what causes diabetes. Diabetes is serious and must be treated. High blood sugar levels can cause problems with your eyes, heart and feet. Talk to your doctor so you can get the information you need to be healthy.

B. Matching Activity. Match the words with the correct definitions.
1. reduce (verb)
2. hormone (noun)
3. risk (noun)
4. glucose (noun)
5. insulin (noun)
6. serious (adj)
7. ethnic (adj)

a. related to race or culture
b. the main type of sugar in the blood
c. a hormone produced in the body to control the amount of sugar in the blood
d. important because of possible danger
e. make less
f. a chemical in the body that travels to other parts of the body to help control how cells and organs work
g. possibility or chance of danger, loss or injury

C. Cloze Activity. Fill in the blanks with the words from B.
1. Lina met other students her class from the same _____ group.
2. Roberto would like to _____ his weight so he walks to school every day.
3. Don't run across the street. There is a _____ that you could get hit by a car.
4. Sugar in the blood is called _____ .
5. Driving a car without a license is _____ problem.
6. _____ controls the amount of sugar in your blood.
7. We have many _____ that help the cells in our bodies.

D. Ordering Activity. Put these sentences into the correct order.
__ Glucose travels in the blood to give our bodies energy.
__ Our bodies change food into glucose.
__ The hormone called insulin moves glucose through our bodies.
__ We eat food.

Part 4: Types of Diabetes
A. Read Passage 2.

Type 1 diabetes
Type 1 diabetes occurs when your body cannot make any insulin. It is most common in children and young adults. People with type 1 diabetes must take insulin. No one knows why people develop type 1 diabetes.

Gestational diabetes
This type of diabetes occurs during pregnancy. The mother's body cannot produce enough insulin while the baby is growing. After the baby is born, the mother's blood glucose levels will usually return to normal. However, these mothers are at greater risk for gestational diabetes in

© Patrice Palmer

their next pregnancy. They are also at risk for developing type 2 diabetes in the future.

Type 2 diabetes
Food gives your body glucose and to use this glucose, your body needs insulin. Insulin is a hormone that helps your body to control the level of glucose in your blood. Type 2 diabetes occurs when your body does not make enough insulin, or your body has trouble using the insulin it makes. Without enough insulin or trouble using insulin, glucose builds up in your blood instead of being used for energy.

B. Reading Comprehension. Answer the questions based on Passage 2. Then check your answers with a partner.
1. What type of diabetes can occur during pregnancy?
_____
2. What type of diabetes can occur if you are a young child?
_____
3. What hormone keeps your blood sugar normal?
_____

Part 5: Risk Factors
A risk factor means that a person may have a greater chance of developing type 2 diabetes.
Risk factors for type 2 diabetes include:
- ethnic background (Asian, South Asian, African-Caribbean, Hispanic, Aboriginals)
- age (over 40 years old)
- family history of diabetes
- weight
- diet
- physical activity
- history of gestational diabetes
- Some risk factors can be changed and other risk factors cannot be changed.

Write down four risk factors that you can change, and four risk factors that you cannot change.

Part 6: Discussion
Discuss the following questions with a classmate. Your teacher will discuss the answers the answers with the whole class.
1. What type of diabetes do you think is the most common? Why?
2. What can a person to reduce the risks of developing type 2 diabetes?
3. What can you do with the information that you learned today?
4. The most important information I learned today was …
5. I still have questions about …

Part 7: Personal Action Plan
Write down one thing that you can do in the next week to be healthier? Make sure that it is something that you are able to do (e.g. walk to school every day).

Post-test
1. There are different types of diabetes.   TRUE / FALSE
2. Diabetes is serious.   TRUE / FALSE
3. Only old people get type 2 diabetes.   TRUE / FALSE
4. Type 2 diabetes is increasing in Canada and around the world.   TRUE / FALSE
5. Some ethnic groups are at high risk for developing diabetes.   TRUE / FALSE
6. People who are overweight are at high risk for developing diabetes.   TRUE / FALSE

© Patrice Palmer

Appendix 2

In order to internationalise the scope of this book as much as possible, we sent out questionnaires to gain further insight into the ESOL context and ESOL materials design outside the UK. My thanks to the numerous ESOL/ESL practitioners who responded: many had produced *EFL* materials for foreign students (the issue of terminology was discussed earlier in this book) and so were not directly relevant here. The process put me in touch with Patrice Palmer in Canada, whose lesson plan is attached in Appendix 1. And I received two completed questionnaires from materials developers in the US, who have that rare combination of experience in publishing materials and experience of teaching immigrants and refugees. I attach their responses here.

How to Write ESOL Materials Questionnaire: Heide Spruck Wrigley

Heide Spruck Wrigley is a US-based senior researcher with Literacywork International. She works nationally and internationally on projects focused on English acquisition as part of immigrant integration. She has taught all levels of ESL and works with teachers and administrators to support projects that interest her. Her work exists at the intersection of research, policy and practice and she has written extensively on issues and options in adult language acquisition, including Teacher Guides and textbooks.

How do you refer to the teaching of English to settled and/or newly arrived migrants in your country?
ESL is now officially called ELA (English language acquisition) or EA (English Acquisition). Students are

ELLs – English language learners or ELs – English learners.

How do you consider this provision to be distinct from mainstream English Language Teaching (by which I mean English for Academic Purposes at University level or English as a Foreign Language for foreign students)? Or is provision, in fact, not distinct and migrant learners attend the same classes as foreign students who do not intend to settle?

A much greater emphasis on preparing students for opportunities or life circumstances that exist locally; emphasis on navigating systems (health, education, police); strong emphasis on immigrant integration (civic, linguistic, economic). Emphasis on community engagement and preparation for local jobs and training in fields that are considered demand occupations in a the region where the program operates; content of instruction is much more localized, particularly at the lower levels; focus on cross-cultural competence needed to navigate between home and community culture and wider US culture.

Please give a bit of background about where you teach/taught ESOL. Please include information about the teaching and learning setting, typical learner profiles in terms of nationalities, educational background, immigration status, reasons for learning English, etc. and any other factors or issues that you think are relevant.

I don't teach ESL currently but work providing Technical Assistance to states (Texas, Indiana, Georgia) and municipalities (City of Seattle) and ELA programs (Carlos Rosario International Public Charter School) and non-profit agencies and institutions (OneAmerica; Migration Policy Institute) and a union (Service Employees International Unit). My focus is on immigrants and refugees still learning English with a strong emphasis on adults who have not had the opportunity for schooling up to or beyond high school; been involved in all levels and contexts for adult ELA (civics, family literacy, work based ESL; vocational technical; academic, transitions to work and training).

What types of ESOL materials have you written?
Issue Briefs; Book Chapters; Position Papers; Textbooks; Hand-book for Teachers; contributed to Program Guide on Contextualizing Instruction
Currently developing a 12-hour online course on Preparing English Learners for Work and Career Pathways for the Department of Education

Could you describe your approach to developing ESOL/ESL materials and if possible outline your writing process?
Literature review; program research and interviews with teachers and learners
Map out topics and themes, integrate scenarios, select meaningful tasks (mostly peer to peer – pairs or small groups); integrate a piece on language structure (how English works) and informal assessments; use the ESL by Design Lesson Flow
literacywork.com/Literacywork.com/ESL_by_Design.html
It also forms the backbone for English Forward.

Here are the materials I developed for the Coalition for the Limited Speaking Elderly: *clese.org/elder-programs/bright-ideas/esl-curriculum*

I don't copyright materials (they are licensed through Creative Commons) but ask that users give credit if they use or adapt the materials.

Do you have national qualifications standards/levels that you can map your resources to?
I'm familiar with levels in the National Reporting System and the College and Career Readiness Standard and refer to those explicitly in PD but not in materials development

Are there other settings in which ESOL teaching takes place in your country? Also, do volunteers deliver ESOL?
Volunteers conduct both one on one and small group instruction using municipal, state or federal funds, in the following settings: Corrections; Libraries; Workplaces; Adult Schools; Community Colleges.

Is there anything else that you would like to add, that you think potential ESOL materials writers need to be aware of, regarding ESOL teaching in your country?
The wide diversity of learners – including those with interrupted schooling and very low levels of literacy who need special support.
More educated adults can often move faster and have academic background knowledge that should be mined. Opportunities that combine face to face with independent learning so students can be part of a community but still practice at their own pace.

HOW TO WRITE ESOL MATERIALS QUESTIONNAIRE:
JANET ISSERLIS

Janet Isserlis has worked with adult immigrants and refugees since 1980. She works with adult literacy practitioners and learners to expand professional learning opportunities, and to support teaching and learning for adults across Rhode Island. She also works with university student programs combining literacy, adult learning and the arts. In addition to classroom work, she is a co-author of *Making Connections: A Literacy and EAL Curriculum from a Feminist Perspective*, a number of articles about language/literacy learning, assessment and practitioner research, and a 1999–2000 Literacy Leadership fellow of the National Institute for Literacy. If you would like to get in touch with Janet, please contact her at *janet.isserlis@gmail.com*

How do you refer to the teaching of English to settled and/or newly arrived migrants in your country?
I use the term ESOL. For many, ESOL is the preferred term as it does not assume that learners are necessarily taking on a second language (for many language learners, English is a third, fourth or even fifth language); it also shifts a sometimes invisible emphasis of the importance of English over that of other languages towards an explicit acknowledgement of the primacy of language and culture in all our lives.

How do you consider this provision to be distinct from mainstream English Language Teaching (by which I mean English for Academic Purposes at University level or English as a Foreign Language for foreign students)? Or is provision, in fact, not distinct and migrant learners attend the same classes as foreign students who do not intend to settle?
The sort of ESOL provision we provide here in Rhode Island (in the northeastern US) – and that many adult educators offer across the US – is designed to meet the strengths and needs of learners whose prior experience with formal education spans the range of little to no prior learning, little to no first language/mother tongue literacy to professionals needing recertification or a translation of/re-gaining of existing credentials. Most of my direct teaching work has been with very basic level literacy. We offer programs that are funded through the federal and state governments and which, accordingly, require pre/post

testing (using state/federal approved standardized instruments).

Courses for visitors or professionals (EFL) tend to be far more lucrative than 'regular' ESOL provision because those offering the classes charge steep tuition and those taking them have some significant sources of income at their disposal.

Please could you give a bit of background about where you teach/taught ESOL. Please include information about the teaching and learning setting, typical learner profiles in terms of nationalities, educational background, immigration status, reasons for learning English, etc. and any other factors or issues that you think are relevant.
Most of my direct teaching work has been with learners at very basic levels of language and literacy. For 12 years I worked with refugees from southeast Asia, Russia and Africa within a community-based English Language center in Providence. In addition to the students I was teaching, the centre also offered ESOL classes to immigrants from Central America, Eastern Europe, countries in Africa and China. Most of the immigrant learners were working; refugees, initially, were funded (in the 1980s) for three years through the Refugee Act of 1980 – allowing for time for school, training and settlement. That has of course almost disappeared so that people now arriving as refugees have – I believe? – 90 days, if that, of cash assistance, help with housing and some job development/language learning support.

Could you describe your approach to developing ESOL/ESL materials and if possible outline your writing process? What types of ESOL materials have you written?
Materials for learners generally come from copying/typing up their words and then developing questions or extension exercises focusing on whatever it is we need to work on.

I've developed a number of follow up texts to language experience writings, and this piece in Bright Ideas delineates the processes of generating and utilising learner-generated content: *brown.edu/Departments/Swearer_Center/Literacy_Resources/brightideas.pdf*
The piece on learner generated writing is designed for practitioners, and is more applicable to classroom practice every day.

Co-wrote a learners' text, Conversations in English, with Linda Mrowicki (Linmore Press).

Some materials – for professional development mostly – including digests about trauma and learning *cal.org/caela/esl_resources/digests/trauma2.html*

and workplace ESL
cal.org/caela/esl_resources/digests/workplacelit.html

These are written to support practitioners' understandings of learners' needs, strengths and challenges. Some of these works were commissioned by publishers, others grew out of colleagues' requests for information and/or my own interest in encoding the work we do so that we can share it round and strengthen it collectively. Additional link shared for this updated edition: *literacyresourcesri.org*

Do you have national qualifications standards/levels that you can map your resources to?
We do. I don't particularly do that as I'm not accountable in that way for materials use/development. A number of the sets of standards in use at the moment across the US are gathered here: *brown.edu/Departments/Swearer_Center/Literacy_Resources/standards.html*

Are there other settings in which ESOL teaching takes place in your country?
In the US, generally, programs are funded through federal and then state streams (which leave us accountable through standardized tests to show progress); through voluntary agencies that might also have similar constraints if they accept state/federal funds); and through worksite specific programs, funded through workforce development entities.

Is there anything else that you would like to add, that you think potential ESOL materials writers need to be aware of, regarding ESOL teaching in your country?
I would say that we need to be aware particularly of learners with limited L1 literacy or formal prior education and of teachers who cycle in and out of the work and need support – not dumbing down, but materials that are flexible and usable in different ways. This is essentially why I almost never use commercially produced materials – they're too grammar-based or oddly specific in contexts and content that is not remotely useful or relevant to learners at basic levels.

This book also exists as an eBook. Other titles in this series are ...

How ELT Publishing Works
How To Plan A Book
How To Write And Deliver Talks
How To Write Audio and Video Scripts*
How To Write Corporate Training Materials
How To Write Critical Thinking Activities*
How To Write EAP Materials
How To Write ESP Materials
How To Write Exam Preparation Materials
How To Write Film And Video Activities
How To Write For Digital Media
How To Write Graded Readers
How To Write Primary Materials
How To Write Reading and Listening Activities*
How To Write Speaking Activities*
How To Write Teacher's Books
How To Write Vocabulary Presentations And Practice*
How To Write Worksheets
How To Write Writing Activities*

Our other paperbacks

How To Write Reading and Listening Activities
How To Write Excellent ELT Materials: The Skills Series
(This title is a compendium containing the six titles asterisked in the list above.)

For further information, contact us via our website at
eltteacher2writer.co.uk

Printed in Great Britain
by Amazon